SO-AGM-366

ONE YEAR
of
Healthy, Hearty & Simple

ONE-DISH MEALS

Revised

365 Low-Fat, Fat-Free, Delicious and Time-Saving Recipes

Pam Spaude & Jan Owan-McMenamin, R.D.

CHRONIMED
PUBLISHING

One Year of Healthy, Hearty & Simple One-Dish Meals, Revised.
© 1996 by Pam Spaude

All rights reserved. Except for brief passages for review purposes, no part of this publication may be reproduced, stored in a retrieval system, or transmitted, in any form or by any means, electronic, photocopying, recording, or otherwise, without the prior written permission of Chronimed Publishing.

Library of Congress Cataloging-in-Publication Data

Spaude Pam.
    One year of healthy, hearty & simple one-dish meals: 365 low-fat, fat-free, delicious, and time-saving recipes / Pam Spaude and Jan Owan-McMenamin.
    p. cm.
    Includes index
    ISBN 1-56561-102-0 ; $14.95
       1. Low-fat diet. 2. Low-cholesterol diet. 3. Casserole cookery.
       4. Diabetes-Diet therapy-Recipes. I. Owan-McMenamin, Jan.
II. Title
RM237.7.S631993
641.5'638-dc20   93-16903
CIP

Edited by: Patricia Richter and Nancy Rothbauer
Cover Design: Terry Dugan Design
Text Design: Liana Raudys
Art/Production Manager: Claire Lewis
Printed in the United States of America

Published by:
Chronimed Publishing, Inc.
P.O. Box 59032
Minneapolis, MN 55459-9686

TABLE OF CONTENTS

NOTICE: CONSULT YOUR HEALTH CARE PROFESSIONAL

Readers are advised to seek the guidance of a licensed physician or health care professional before making any changes in prescribed health care regimens, as each individual case or need may vary. This book is intended for informational purposes only and is not for use as an alternative to appropriate medical care. While every effort has been made to ensure that the information is the most current available, new research findings, being released with increasing frequency, may invalidate some data.

INTRODUCTION

The original edition of this book was designed to help you cook simple healthful meals that taste good, are nutritious, and are quick and easy to prepare. Our objective hasn't changed for this revised edition, but we have added and improved more than a month's worth of recipes.

Today it seems we are all more aware of the relationship between health and diet, so we look for ways to cook meals that are low in cholesterol, fat and sodium. This book is filled with recipes to help you cook healthfully. In fact, for this revised edition, we've added easy-to-spot icons that will help you find low-fat and nonfat main dish meals.

Our collection provides a main dish meal for every day of the year, and to complete the menu nutritionally, we have suggested some side dishes that complement the entrée.

Each of our recipes includes the nutritional analysis and exchange information that lets you see for yourself exactly which components are part of the main dish. You can add your own choices to our main dishes, or add nothing, remembering that one meal does not necessarily have to satisfy your entire day's worth of nutritional components, or exchanges. The American Diabetes Association and The American Dietetic Association revised their exchange lists and introduced new food groupings since *One Year of Healthy, Hearty & Simple One-Dish Meals* was first published. However, we've chosen to keep the exchanges that are familiar to many people. Not only are they still accurate, but they can be easily translated into the newer exchange groupings.

We hope you'll like this collection. We're sure you'll find most meals quick and easy to prepare. So, happy, healthy eating to you for the next year and for many years to come!

Pam Spaude
Jan Owan-McMenamin

Recipe Notes

Substitutions:
- ⅛ tsp. garlic powder for 1 clove garlic (Note: If you especially like garlic, use bottled garlic, already chopped, such as Polaner)
- margarine for butter
- Miracle Whip salad dressing for mayonnaise

Measures:
- dash or pinch = less than 1/8 tsp.
- 1 cup uncooked rice = 3 to 4 cups cooked

Abbreviations:
- tsp. = teaspoon
- Tbsp. = tablespoon
- pkg. = package

Miscellaneous:
Use whole-wheat breads and pasta, and whole-grain rice whenever possible for improved nutrition in your meals.

Recipes are considered low fat or nonfat according to the guidelines set by the Food and Drug Administration:
  nonfat = contains less than 0.5 grams of fat per serving
  low fat = contains 3 grams or less per serving

Definitions

baste to moisten food while it is cooking

blanch to scald briefly in hot water

blend to mix smoothly and inseparably together (only if specified in the recipe does it mean using an electric blender)

confectioner's sugar powdered sugar

cream to mix or beat into a creamy, smooth consistency

diced cut into small cubes

dry mustard powdered form of the spice

garnish to add something to a food dish that provides color and/or decoration or distinctive flavor

julienne cut into thin strips

marinate to soak meat in a seasoned liquid before cooking

minced cut or chopped into very fine pieces

parboil to boil partially, not to doneness

pasta a food paste, dried into different shapes such as spaghetti, macaroni, noodles, etc.

prepared mustard the paste form of this spice; usually used as a sandwich condiment

purée to make into a mushy, almost soupy consistency

salad dressing can be synonymous with a Miracle Whip type product, as opposed to mayonnaise, which is not advertised as "salad dressing"

sauté to fry lightly with a little oil, usually just to beginning of tenderness, not crispiness

score to make shallow cuts, usually crisscrossed

shortening a solidified fat such as Crisco

simmer to cook at or just below the boiling point

whisk to whip or beat with a hand utensil

Salads

1 7½-oz. can water-packed tuna
1 16-oz. can garbanzo beans, drained
⅔ cup chopped celery

⅔ cup chopped onion
⅔ cup chopped green pepper
¼ cup chopped red pepper
1 cup chopped carrots
1 large tomato, chopped
1 tsp. minced garlic
1 tsp. dried parsley flakes, crushed
⅔ cup low-cal Italian dressing
5 cups shredded lettuce
1 cup sliced mushrooms

Combine all ingredients in a large bowl and toss lightly until mixed well.

Per serving
202 calories
10 mg cholesterol
504 mg sodium
0.15 gm saturated fat
1.2 gm fat

Exchanges per serving
1 bread
1 meat
1 vegetable

On the side Honeydew melon cut into slices or served in a cup as melon balls adds a refreshing taste and completes this meal nutritionally.

1¾ cup cooked long-grain rice
1 10-oz. package frozen peas, thawed
1¾ cup freshly cooked or drained, canned black beans
1½ Tbsp. vegetable oil
⅓ cup chopped pimentos
1 tsp. Dijon-style mustard
1½ Tbsp. ketchup
¼ cup red wine vinegar
⅛ tsp. pepper
6 lettuce leaves

Place rice, peas and black beans in a mixing bowl. In a blender, combine the remaining ingredients, except the lettuce, and blend. Toss with the rice, peas and beans. Chill covered for 2 hours. Serve on lettuce leaves.

Per serving
204 calories
0 mg cholesterol
241 mg. sodium
0.5 gm saturated fat
3.5 gm fat

Exchanges per serving
2 bread
1 vegetable

On the side Serve with fresh pears and a glass of low-fat milk and you have a nutritionally complete meal.

2½ cups fresh bean sprouts
¼ cup sliced water chestnuts
     ½ cup sliced seedless grapes

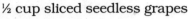

     1 diced medium peach
     ⅓ cup diced green pepper
     ½ cup cooked rice
     ⅓ cup plain low-fat yogurt
1 tsp. curry powder
1 tsp. soy sauce

Combine bean sprouts, chestnuts, grapes, peach, green pepper and rice. In a small bowl, mix yogurt, curry powder, and soy sauce. Pour dressing over salad. Toss and serve.

Per serving
75 calories
0.5 mg cholesterol
597 mg sodium
0.75 gm saturated fat
0.5 gm fat

Exchanges per serving
1 fruit
½ vegetable

On the side A fresh peach per person complements this salad and adds only 40 calories and one fruit exchange. One slice of bread or a small roll and a cup of milk make this a complete meal.

Broccoli and Cauliflower Salad

2 cups broccoli florets, steamed
2 cups cauliflower, steamed
4 Tbsp. unsalted sunflower seeds
½ cup raisins
2 Tbsp. light mayonnaise
6 Tbsp. plain low-fat yogurt
1 Tbsp. honey
2 Tbsp. lemon juice
½ tsp. minced garlic

In a salad bowl, combine broccoli, cauliflower, sunflower seeds and raisins. In a small bowl, mix mayonnaise, yogurt, honey, lemon juice and garlic. Blend well. Pour over broccoli-cauliflower mixture. Toss and chill.

Per serving
193 calories
3 mg cholesterol
51 mg sodium
1.1 gm saturated fat
6 gm fat

Exchanges per serving
1 fat
1 fruit
2 vegetable

On the side An 8-ounce glass of milk or 1 slice of bread makes this meal nutritionally complete.

Dressing:

1 cup skim milk
     2 Tbsp. cornstarch
     ½ tsp. mustard
     2 Tbsp. vinegar
     ⅛ tsp. salt

Salad:

2 cups shredded cabbage
1 cup shredded carrots
¼ cup finely chopped fresh parsley
¼ cup chopped onion
1 Tbsp. finely cut chives
1 tsp. lemon juice

Mix all dressing ingredients in a small bowl. Blend well and set aside.

In a bowl, combine cabbage, carrots, parsley, onions and chives; mix. Pour lemon juice over mixture. Add dressing to taste; toss.

Per serving
29 calories
0.9 mg cholesterol
85 mg sodium
0 gm saturated fat
0 gm fat

Exchanges per serving
1 vegetable

On the side Serve with fresh pears, a slice of bread and 8 ounces milk to complete the meal.

Carrot and Raisin Salad

4 cups grated carrots
1⅓ cup canned crushed pineapple
   (unsweetened juice)
½ cup raisins
2 tsp. lemon juice
⅔ cup low-fat plain yogurt
3 Tbsp. light mayonnaise
2 Tbsp. shredded coconut
2 tsp. sugar

In a bowl, combine carrots, pineapple, raisins and lemon juice; toss. In a small bowl, combine remaining ingredients; use a hand mixer to beat until blended well. Pour over carrot mixture and toss until salad is well coated. Chill for 1 hour.

Per serving
191 calories
3 mg cholesterol
89 mg sodium
1.4 gm saturated fat
3.3 gm fat

Exchanges per serving
1 fat
1 fruit
½ skim milk
1 vegetable

On the side Serve with low-fat plain yogurt and the meal is nutritionally complete.

⅔ cup light mayonnaise
¼ cup mustard
    2 Tbsp. vinegar
    ½ tsp. garlic powder
    ¼ tsp. ground red pepper
    ¼ cup diced onion
    4 cups cooked cavatelli pasta
1 cup diced celery
1 cup chopped green pepper
1 cup chopped red pepper

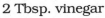

In a large bowl, combine mayonnaise, mustard, vinegar and spices. Add remaining ingredients; toss well. Cover and chill.

Per serving
134 calories
1.6 mg cholesterol
120 mg sodium
0.65 gm saturated fat
2 gm fat

Exchanges per serving
1 bread
1 fat

On the side Serve with your choice of vegetable salad, a fruit, and a cup of skim milk to complete the meal.

2 cups cooked chicken breast halves without skin,
   cubed
1 15-oz. can garbanzo beans, drained
¾ cup lowfat cheddar cheese, cubed
¾ cup sliced celery
¾ cup chopped green pepper
⅛ cup sliced green onions
½ cup light mayonnaise
1½ Tbsp. lime juice
¼ tsp garlic powder
¼ tsp. chili powder
6 lettuce leaves

In a bowl, combine chicken, garbanzo beans, cheese, celery, green pepper, and green onions. Stir together mayonnaise, lime juice, garlic powder, and chili powder. Stir into chicken mixture, toss. Chill. Serve on lettuce leaves.

Per serving
270 calories
40 mg cholesterol
366 mg sodium
1.3 gm saturated fat
15 gm fat

Exchanges per serving
1 bread
1 fat
3 meat

On the side This salad is nearly a nutritionally complete meal all alone. Add a glass of milk and a fruit for dessert and you have it all.

2 cups boneless, skinned, cooked chicken breasts,
    diced
20 small red seedless grapes, cut into halves
2 apples, diced
⅔ cup diced celery
⅔ cup diced onion
3 Tbsp. light mayonnaise
2 tsp. vinegar
4 tsp. lemon juice
⅛ tsp. black pepper

In a mixing bowl, combine all ingredients and toss
well. Refrigerate until thoroughly chilled, then serve.

Per serving
255 calories
87 mg cholesterol
103 mg sodium
2.6 gm saturated fat
21.5 gm fat

Exchanges per serving
½ fat
1 fruit
2 meat

On the side A cold vegetable, such as asparagus spears
vinaigrette, a small dinner roll, or a small tossed salad will
complete this meal.

Chicken Pecan Salad

Serves 4 **10**

1¾ cup chopped cooked chicken
2 Tbsp. chopped pecans
⅓ cup diced celery
3 Tbsp. grated carrots
½ cup plain low-fat yogurt
½ tsp. chopped dillweed
⅛ tsp. salt
⅛ tsp. pepper
4 lettuce leaves

Combine chicken, pecans, celery and carrots. Toss with yogurt, dillweed, salt and pepper. Serve on lettuce leaves.

Per serving
344 calories
179 mg cholesterol
271 mg sodium
4.5 gm saturated fat
14 gm fat

Exchanges per serving
1 fat
3 meat
½ milk
1 vegetable

On the side Serve with a fresh peach per person, a slice of bread, or a small roll for a complete meal.

11   Chicken Raspberry Salad

Dressing:

1 cup nonfat plain yogurt
½ cup fresh or loosely packed, frozen raspberries
1 Tbsp. raspberry or red wine vinegar
1 tsp. sugar

Blend all dressing ingredients in blender until smooth, about 15 seconds.

Salad:

4 cups bite-sized pieces of mixed salad greens
2 cups cut-up, cooked chicken
1 cup fresh or loosely packed, frozen raspberries
⅓ cup thinly sliced celery
¼ cup toasted sliced almonds

Toss salad greens, chicken, raspberries, and celery. Sprinkle with almonds. Serve with raspberry dressing on the side.

Per serving
250 calories
60 mg cholesterol
130 mg sodium
2.4 gm saturated fat
11 gm fat

Exchanges per serving
½ fat
1 fruit
2 meat

On the side Add a small muffin, some carrot sticks, and a glass of low-fat milk to complete your meal.

Chickpea Vegetable Salad

Serves 4 **12**

2 cups tomatoes, cubed
1½ cup chopped carrots
⅔ cup chopped celery
2 cups chopped green pepper
2 cups cooked chickpeas
1 Tbsp. vegetable oil
4 Tbsp. lime juice
1 tsp. Dijon-style mustard
1½ tsp. mint flakes or leaves
½ tsp. honey
1 tsp. vinegar
⅛ tsp. black pepper
4 lettuce leaves

In a large mixing bowl, combine tomatoes, carrots, celery, green pepper and chickpeas. In a small bowl, combine oil, lime juice, mustard, mint flakes, honey, vinegar and black pepper; mix and blend well. Pour over chickpeas and vegetables; toss. Cover and chill 1 hour. Serve on lettuce leaves.

Per serving
201 calories
0 mg cholesterol
219 mg sodium
1.3 gm saturated fat
3.5 gm fat

Exchanges per serving
2 bread
1 vegetable

On the side Serve with fresh cantaloupe and a glass of milk for a nutritionally complete meal.

¾ cup canned pineapple, no sugar added
1 Tbsp. apple cider vinegar
1 Tbsp. light soy sauce
1 Tbsp. Dijon-style mustard
2 tsp. vegetable oil
⅛ tsp. ground ginger
1 cup boneless, skinned, cooked chicken breast, cut
    into thin strips
2 cups shredded lettuce
⅓ cup diced green onions
1 Tbsp. finely chopped red pepper
¼ cup water chestnuts, sliced
½ tsp. sesame seed

In a glass bowl, combine juice from pineapple, vinegar, soy sauce, mustard, oil and ginger. Add chicken and toss to coat. Cover and refrigerate 1 hour. In another bowl, combine lettuce, green onions, pineapple, red pepper and water chestnuts; mix and toss. Add chicken mixture to lettuce mixture; toss. Sprinkle with sesame seeds.

Per serving
304 calories
85 mg cholesterol
589 mg sodium
2.15 gm saturated fat
11.98 gm fat

Exchanges per serving
1 fat
1 fruit
2½ meat

On the side Serve with a slice of your favorite bread and a glass of milk for a nutritionally complete meal.

Cold Noodle Salad

8 oz. dry vermicelli
1 tsp. minced garlic
¼ cup vegetable oil
½ cup lemon juice
1 Tbsp. soy sauce
2 small cucumbers, sliced
2 cups shredded cabbage
2 potatoes, boiled, peeled and cubed
⅛ tsp. pepper

Cook vermicelli according to directions on package; drain and rinse with cold water.

In a bowl, mix garlic, oil, lemon juice and soy sauce. Add vermicelli, cucumber, cabbage and potatoes; mix well. Season with pepper.

Per serving
311 calories
0 mg cholesterol
143.6 mg sodium
1.16 gm saturated fat
10.3 gm fat

Exchanges per serving
2 bread
2 fat
1 vegetable

On the side Serve with a glass of a glass of milk and a piece of your favorite fruit.

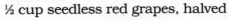

3 cups shredded cabbage
1 orange, peeled and sectioned, cut in half
    1 tangerine, peeled and sectioned, cut in half
    ½ cup seedless red grapes, halved
    ½ cup seedless green grapes, halved
    ¼ cup sliced celery
    1 apple, cored and chopped
1 8-oz. carton low-fat orange yogurt
⅛ tsp. nutmeg
⅓ cup sunflower seeds

In a large salad bowl, combine cabbage, orange pieces, tangerine pieces, red grapes, green grapes, celery, and apple. Combine yogurt and nutmeg. Pour yogurt mixture over cabbage and fruit; toss. Sprinkle with sunflower seeds. Chill.

Per serving
88 calories
0 mg cholesterol
10.8 mg sodium
0.3 gm saturated fat
2.9 gm fat

Exchanges per serving
1 fruit
½ skim milk

On the side Serve with your favorite bread or rolls.

1 cup long grain rice
2 cups fresh orange juice
1½ 4-oz. jars pimentos, drained and cut into strips
1 small red onion, minced
½ lb. snow peas, trimmed
3 medium oranges, peeled and divided into sections,
    and cut up

Dressing:

1 tsp. mustard
juice of ½ lemon
3 Tbsp. balsamic vinegar
4 Tbsp. light extra virgin olive oil
2 tsp. minced garlic
salt and pepper to taste

Mix the mustard, lemon juice, and vinegar. Gradually
stir in the olive oil. Stir in garlic and season to taste
with salt and pepper. Let stand for 20 minutes before
using. Rinse the rice and put into sauce pan with
orange juice. Bring to a boil. Stir, then cover and cook
on low until the liquid is absorbed and rice is tender.
Fluff with fork, cool. Mix together the prepared vegetables and fold into the cooled rice. Mix the oranges into
the rice, and toss thoroughly with the dressing.

Per serving
249 calories
0 mg cholesterol
16.5 mg sodium
1.3 gm saturated fat
9 gm fat

Exchanges per serving
2 bread
1 vegetable
2 fat
1 fruit

On the side Serve with honeydew, ⅓ melon or 1 cup per person.
Add a glass of milk to complete the meal.

1¾ cup cooked long-grain rice
2½ cup freshly cooked green beans, cut in 2-inch
   lengths
1¾ cup 96% fat-free ham, diced
½ cup chili sauce
¼ cup red wine vinegar
⅛ tsp. pepper
¼ cup rice bran
6 lettuce leaves

In a mixing bowl, combine rice, green beans and ham.
In a blender, combine chili sauce, vinegar and pepper;
blend. Toss dressing with the rice mixture. Chill for 2
hours, covered. Add rice bran and toss just before
serving. Serve on lettuce leaves.

Per serving
230 calories
25.3 mg cholesterol
971 mg sodium
1.03 gm saturated fat
5.1 gm fat

Exchanges per serving
1 bread
2 meat
1 vegetable

On the side Serve with fresh fruit.

Lentil Turkey Salad

¾ cup lentils, rinsed
1½ cups cooked turkey, cubed
⅛ cup sliced black olives
⅓ cup green peppers, chopped
⅓ cup chopped red peppers
½ cup sliced onions
1½ tsp. curry powder
1 tsp. vegetable oil
1½ Tbsp. light mayonnaise
2 Tbsp. plain low-fat yogurt

Place lentils in a saucepan and cover with water. Cook lentils on low heat for 20 to 25 minutes. Drain and rinse with cold water. In a bowl, mix with remaining ingredients. Toss and chill.

Per serving
240 calories
31 mg cholesterol
73 mg sodium
0.92 gm saturated fat
4.2 gm fat

Exchanges per serving
½ bread
1 fat
2 meat

On the side Serve with plain low-fat yogurt, 1 cup per person, on fresh vegetables, or a fresh fruit of your choice.

19 Macaroni Salad

2 cups cooked elbow macaroni
1 cup diced celery
1 cup diced carrots
⅓ cup diced green pepper
¼ cup diced green onions
½ cup peas
1 Tbsp. Dijon-style mustard
½ cup light mayonnaise

Combine macaroni, celery, carrots, green pepper, onions and peas in a bowl; toss. Mix mustard and mayonnaise; pour over macaroni salad and toss.

Per serving
188 calories
2 mg cholesterol
135 mg sodium
1 gm saturated fat
5 gm fat

Exchanges per serving
1 bread
1 fat
1 vegetable

On the side Serve with cantaloupe, ⅛ melon or 1 cup per person, and a glass of milk for a nutritionally complete meal.

1½ cup small shell macaroni
⅔ cup chopped onions

10 oz. package frozen mixed vegetables

¾ cup low-fat cottage cheese
¼ cup low-fat yogurt
1½ tsp. Worcestershire sauce
¾ tsp. dry mustard

1 cup chopped carrots
½ cup chopped green peppers
¼ cup chopped red peppers
¼ cup chopped celery
⅛ cup chopped radishes

Cook macaroni and onion in boiling water according to package directions; drain and rinse with cold water. Cook vegetables and drain. Add cooked vegetables to macaroni and onion and chill for 15 minutes in freezer. Purée cottage cheese, yogurt, Worcestershire sauce, and mustard in blender until smooth. Add yogurt mixture and all remaining ingredients to chilled macaroni mixture. Toss until well blended.

Per serving
180 calories
1.28 mg cholesterol
135 mg sodium
0.28 gm saturated fat
1.3 gm fat

Exchanges per serving
1 bread
1 meat
1 vegetable

On the side Serve with fresh pears for a refreshing complement to this salad.

21 Multicolor Bean Salad

Serves 6

2 16-oz. cans of mixed beans such as navy beans, red
beans or cooked black-eyed peas
½ lb. green beans, trimmed
6 green onions, chopped
small bunch of fresh parsley, finely chopped

Garlic dressing:
1 Tbsp. lemon juice
4 Tbsp. wine vinegar
1 tsp. salt
3 cloves of garlic, minced
1 tsp. black pepper
½ cup light extra virgin olive oil

Drain and rinse the canned beans. Drain thoroughly.
Steam the green beans until tender, 5 to 6 minutes.
Toss all the beans together with green onions. To
make the dressing, mix together the lemon juice, vinegar, salt, garlic, and pepper. Stirring all the time, add
the olive oil. Add the garlic dressing to the beans and
toss. Sprinkle with the chopped parsley.

Per serving
359 calories
0 mg cholesterol
822 mg sodium
2.6 gm saturated fat
19 gm fat

Exchanges per serving
2 bread
3½ fat
1 vegetable

On the side Serve with fresh fruit and a glass of milk to complete
the meal.

Pasta and Bell Pepper Salad

½ lb. bow tie pasta
1 red bell pepper, cut in thin slices
1 yellow bell pepper, cut in thin slices
7 oz. green beans, cooked
1 cup red kidney beans
¼ cup chopped fresh parsley
2 Tbsp. fresh basil leaves
1 oz. Romano cheese

Lemon dressing:
juice of 1 lemon
2 Tbsp. soy sauce
5 Tbsp. sesame oil
1 tsp. grated fresh ginger
1 clove garlic, minced
¼ tsp. black pepper

For dressing: mix all the ingredients together in a small bowl. Cook the pasta according to package directions. Drain and rinse under cold water in a colander. Mix the pasta, bell peppers, green beans, kidney beans, and parsley in a salad bowl. Add the lemon dressing and toss until mixed together. Fold in the basil and garnish with the Romano cheese.

Per serving
351 calories
4 mg cholesterol
601 mg sodium
2 gm saturated fat
13.6 gm fat

Exchanges per serving
2½ bread
1 vegetable
2 fat

On the side Serve with a fresh peach for a complete meal.

6 oz. rigatoni
2½ cups chopped tomatoes
⅓ cup feta cheese
⅓ cup low-cal Italian dressing
½ cup chopped green onions
⅛ cup sliced pitted black olives
6 cups torn, fresh spinach
⅛ tsp. pepper

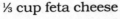

Cook pasta according to package directions; drain.
Combine pasta and remaining ingredients. Toss to
coat.

Per serving
123 calories
6.25 mg cholesterol
196 mg sodium
1.17 gm saturated fat
2.87 gm fat

Exchanges per serving
1 bread
½ fat
1 vegetable

On the side You can increase the nutritional content of this salad
by adding more cheese, or serve with an 8 ounce glass of milk
and a fresh fruit to complete the meal.

Potato Broccoli Salad

24

5 medium potatoes
1 bunch broccoli
¼ cup vegetable oil
¼ cup lime juice
½ tsp. garlic powder
1¼ tsp. basil
⅛ tsp. Tabasco sauce
¼ cup onions, chopped

Peel and cook potatoes until tender; then dice them. Wash broccoli and break into small florets. Steam broccoli until tender-crisp. In a small saucepan, combine oil, lime juice, garlic powder, basil, Tabasco sauce and onions. Bring mixture to a boil, stirring all the while. Put potatoes and broccoli in serving bowl. Pour sauce over vegetables; toss gently.

Per serving
180 calories
0 mg cholesterol
53 mg sodium
1.2 gm saturated fat
9.5 gm fat

Exchanges per serving
1 bread
1 fat
1 vegetable

On the side Serve with a glass of milk and a fresh fruit to have a nutritionally complete meal.

2 cups green beans, cut in half
1½ cups fresh peas
2 cups cooked rice
3 cups fresh tomatoes, cubed
½ cup sliced green onions
1 Tbsp. fresh basil
1 tsp. dried parsley flakes, crushed
1½ Tbsp. lemon juice
2½ Tbsp. vegetable oil
2 tsp. safflower oil
1 7 oz. can tuna fish

Steam beans until tender, then cool. Cook peas until tender, then cool. Mix together remaining ingredients. Mix in beans and peas. Toss.

Per serving
267 calories
19 mg cholesterol
469 mg sodium
1.4 gm saturated fat
9.7 gm fat

Exchanges per serving
2 bread
1 fat
1 meat
1 vegetable

On the side Serve with honeydew, ⅓ melon or 1 cup per person. Add a glass of milk to complete the meal.

1 8-oz. package frozen, cooked small shrimp
2 cups frozen peas, thawed
½ cup low-fat plain yogurt
¼ cup light mayonnaise
½ tsp. curry powder
½ tsp. lemon juice
½ tsp. celery seed
⅛ cup green onions, sliced
½ cup chopped celery
1 small tomato, chopped
4 lettuce leaves

Rinse and drain shrimp and peas. In a mixing bowl, stir together yogurt, mayonnaise, curry powder, lemon juice, and celery seed. Add shrimp, peas, onions, celery, and tomatoes. Toss until coated. To serve, line plates with lettuce leaves. Spoon shrimp mixture onto plates.

Per serving
201 calories
83 mg cholesterol
212 mg sodium
0.75 gm saturated fat
5.75 gm fat

Exchanges per serving
½ bread
1 fat
2 meat

On the side Add more vegetables to this recipe to enhance it nutritionally, or serve surrounded with fresh, crunchy vegetables of your choice. Finish off the meal with a refreshing cup of honeydew melon balls.

2 envelopes unflavored gelatin
2 cups skim milk
    1 cup plain nonfat yogurt
    3 Tbsp. vinegar
    1 tsp. salt
    1 tsp. prepared horseradish
    2 4½-oz. cans shrimp, drained
½ cup diced celery
¼ cup chopped green pepper
½ cup diced part-skim American cheese

In 2-quart saucepan, add gelatin and ½ cup milk. Stir until dissolved over low heat. Add remaining milk and remove from heat. Chill until mixture begins to set. Add yogurt, vinegar, salt, and horseradish; mix well. Fold in shrimp, celery, green pepper, and cheese. Pour into 9 x 9-inch pan and chill 3 hours. Cut into 3-inch squares. 1 square = 1 serving.

Per serving
102 calories
60.2 mg cholesterol
391 mg sodium
0.8 gm saturated fat
1.5 gm fat

Exchanges per serving
1 meat
½ skim milk

On the side Serve with cantaloupe, a slice of bread, and a crunchy vegetable salad for a complete meal.

Spinach Fruit Salad

¼ cup vegetable oil
3 Tbsp. red wine vinegar
1 Tbsp. lemon juice
½ tsp. ground ginger
1 lb. fresh spinach
3 cups fresh strawberries, sliced
½ cup part-skim cheddar cheese, shredded

Blend oil, vinegar, lemon juice, and ginger in a large bowl. Add spinach, strawberries and cheese; toss.

Per serving
119 calories
2.3 mg cholesterol
43 mg sodium
1.4 gm saturated fat
10.5 gm fat

Exchanges per serving
1 fat
1 fruit
1 vegetable

On the side Serve with a slice of your favorite fresh bread and a cup of low-fat plain yogurt.

6 oz. fresh spinach
1 15¼-oz. can chunk pineapple in unsweetened juice
4 tsp. cornstarch
½ tsp. ginger
¼ tsp. allspice
⅛ tsp. lemon pepper
12 oz. cooked, smoked turkey sausage
1 Tbsp. lemon juice
2 cups broccoli florets
1 cup sliced red pepper

Clean spinach and tear into bite-size pieces. Drain pineapple and reserve juice. Add water to juice to equal one cup. In a bowl, combine juice mixture, cornstarch, ginger, allspice, and lemon pepper. Set aside. Cut turkey into thin slices. In a large skillet, cook and stir turkey sausage until browned. Stir in pineapple juice mixture, lemon juice, broccoli, and red pepper strips. Cook and stir until thickened; add pineapple and cook through. Cool and toss with spinach in a bowl.

Per serving
218 calories
36 mg cholesterol
935 mg sodium
1.0 gm saturated fat
3.3 gm fat

Exchanges per serving
1 fruit
2 meat
1 vegetable

On the side Serve with a slice of toasted bread and some crunchy fresh vegetables for a complete meal.

Tarragon Shrimp Salad

8 oz. medium-sized cooked shrimp,
   peeled and deveined
5 Tbsp. light mayonnaise
¼ cup sliced green onion
2 tsp. lemon juice
1½ tsp. skim milk
½ tsp. dried tarragon, crushed
⅛ tsp. lemon pepper
⅛ tsp. paprika
2 cups chopped lettuce

Cut shrimp in half lengthwise. In a bowl, combine mayonnaise, green onions, lemon juice, milk, tarragon, lemon pepper, and paprika. Stir shrimp into mixture; cover and chill for 1 hour. Serve on chopped lettuce.

Per serving
184 calories
178 mg cholesterol
221 mg sodium
1.4 gm saturated fat
7.2 gm fat

Exchanges per serving
1 fat
3 meat

On the side Serve with fresh cantaloupe, bread, and crunchy vegetables for a nutritionally complete meal.

1 lb. fresh asparagus, trimmed
4 romaine leaves

4 cups torn romaine
10 cherry tomatoes, halved
⅓ cup prepared fat-free Italian salad dressing
2 Tbsp. grated Parmesan cheese

In a large sauce pan, cook asparagus in boiling water for 5 to 6 minutes or until crisp-tender. Place in ice water to stop cooking. Line an 11 x 7 x 2-inch pan with romaine leaves. Top with torn romaine. Arrange asparagus over the romaine; top with tomatoes. Pour dressing over all. Sprinkle with cheese. Chill for 1 hour.

Per serving
64 calories
2 mg cholesterol
165 mg sodium
0.6 gm saturated fat
2.5 gm fat

Exchanges per serving
2 vegetable

On the side Serve with fresh fruit or a small roll for a complete meal.

1½ cup shredded, cooked turkey
2 bananas, sliced and peeled
⅛ cup chopped celery
⅓ cup chopped carrots
⅛ cup green onions
⅓ cup raisins
⅓ cup light mayonnaise
¼ tsp. cumin
¼ tsp. dill
⅛ tsp. garlic powder
salad greens

Toss together turkey, bananas, celery, carrots, onions and raisins. Combine the mayonnaise, cumin, dill and garlic powder; blend well. Fold into turkey mixture. Refrigerate for 1 hour. Serve on top of salad greens.

Per serving
370 calories
95 mg cholesterol
171 mg sodium
2.9 gm saturated fat
9.2 gm fat

Exchanges per serving
1 fat
1 fruit
3 meat
1 vegetable

On the side Serve with fresh bread to complete the meal.

1 10-oz. can tuna in spring water
⅔ cup chopped celery
½ cup chopped green onions
1 chili pepper, chopped
1 tsp. minced garlic
4 tsp. lemon juice
½ tsp. celery seed
1 Tbsp. soy sauce
2 Tbsp. frozen apple juice concentrate, thawed
1 cup frozen peas, thawed
⅔ cup grated carrots
2 cups cooked rice
1½ tsp. sweet basil
1 tsp. prepared mustard
6 lettuce leaves

Mix all the ingredients except lettuce together in a mixing bowl. Serve on lettuce leaves.

Per serving
151 calories
1 mg cholesterol
497 mg sodium
0.1 gm saturated fat
0.22 gm fat

Exchanges per serving
1 bread
1½ meat

On the side Serve with cantaloupe and a glass of low-fat milk to complete the meal.

Waldorf Salad

Serves 4 **34**

3 Tbsp. lemon juice
3 small red Delicious apples, diced
⅔ cup diced celery
⅓ cup raisins
½ cup shredded carrots
3 Tbsp. light mayonnaise
2 Tbsp. sunflower seeds

In a small bowl, sprinkle lemon juice over apples,
toss. Add celery, raisins, carrots and mayonnaise; mix
until coated. Cover and refrigerate 30 minutes. Before
serving, sprinkle mixture with sunflower seeds.

Per serving
159 calories
1.5 mg cholesterol
33 mg sodium
0.62 gm saturated fat
5.7 gm fat

Exchanges per serving
1½ fat
1 fruit
1 vegetable

On the side Serve with a glass of milk or a cup of plain nonfat
yogurt and a slice of bread.

2 cups skinned and cooked chicken, cubed
⅔ cup low-fat plain yogurt
1 Tbsp. minced onion
½ tsp. curry
⅔ cup diced celery
½ cup water chestnuts, cut
1 cup fresh, sliced mushrooms
3 whole-wheat English muffins, toasted

Preheat oven to 450°F. Mix all ingredients except the muffins together in an 8-inch square baking dish. Bake for 10 to 15 minutes. Cut English muffins in half. Divide mixture evenly on each half.

Per serving
266 calories
73 mg cholesterol
238 mg sodium
1.74 gm saturated fat
5.6 gm fat

Exchanges per serving
1 bread
2 meat
½ skim milk

On the side Serve with green, red and yellow peppers and a fresh fruit for a nutritionally complete meal.

Zesty Chicken Salad

½ cup plain low-fat yogurt
2 Tbsp. light mayonnaise
½ cup lemon juice
¼ cup grated Parmesan cheese
2 tsp. minced garlic
1 lb. boneless, skinned, cooked chicken, cubed
½ cup diced celery
¼ cup diced green onion
⅛ tsp. pepper

In a bowl, combine yogurt, mayonnaise, lemon juice, Parmesan cheese and garlic; blend well. Add chicken, celery, green onion and pepper. Toss well to coat.

Per serving
234 calories
82 mg cholesterol
88 mg sodium
3.0 gm saturated fat
8.37 gm fat

Exchanges per serving
½ bread
1 fat
2 meat

On the side Serve with a vegetable of your choice and top off with fresh honeydew melon slices for dessert.

Soups

½ cup finely chopped onion
4¼ cups water
    1 tsp. minced garlic
    2 Tbsp. tomato sauce
    1½ Tbsp. soy sauce
    1 tsp. Worcestershire sauce
    ½ tsp. black pepper
2 broccoli stalks, florets
2 cups elbow macaroni

In saucepan, cook onions with ¼ cup water until onion is soft. Add garlic and cook for one minute. Add tomato sauce, soy sauce and Worcestershire sauce. Stir well. Add 4 cups water and bring to a boil. Add pepper and broccoli; cook for 5 minutes. Add macaroni and cook for 10 to 15 minutes more.

Per serving
130 calories
0 mg cholesterol
257 mg sodium
0 gm saturated fat
1.02 gm fat

Exchanges per serving
1½ bread
1 vegetable

On the side To make this a nutritionally complete meal, serve with a glass of milk and top off with a fresh fruit of your choice.

1 Tbsp. vegetable oil
⅔ cup finely chopped onions
⅔ cup chopped red peppers
½ cup chopped celery
½ cup bran
½ tsp. cayenne pepper
¾ tsp. garlic powder
6 cups low-sodium chicken broth
2 bay leaves
2 16 oz. cans red beans, drained
1½ lbs. boneless, skinless chicken breasts, cubed

In 8-quart saucepan, heat oil. Add onions, red pepper and celery; sauté and stir constantly. Add bran, cayenne pepper and garlic powder; continue to sauté until bran begins to fill bottom of saucepan and turn brown. Add broth; stir. Add bay leaves and beans; simmer for 30 minutes. Add chicken and cook until chicken is cooked through. Remove bay leaves.

Per serving
287 calories
84 mg cholesterol
240 mg sodium
3.2 gm saturated fat
7.6 gm fat

Exchanges per serving
1 bread
½ fat
2 meat
1 vegetable

On the side To complete this meal, serve fresh fruit for dessert.

1 8-oz. can stewed tomatoes
1 6-oz. can vegetable juice cocktail
    ½ cup chopped green pepper
    1 tsp. minced onion
    ½ tsp. Worcestershire sauce
    ¼ tsp. ground red pepper
    ⅔ cup water
1 6-oz. package frozen, cooked, small shrimp
⅓ cup quick-cooking rice

In saucepan, combine stewed tomatoes, vegetable juice, green pepper, onion, Worcestershire sauce, red pepper, and ⅔ cup water. Bring to a boil. Stir in shrimp and rice. Return to a boil; remove from heat and let stand 5 minutes or until rice is done.

Per serving
176 calories
128 mg cholesterol
541 mg sodium
0 gm saturated fat
1 gm fat

Exchanges per serving
1 bread
1 meat
1 vegetable

On the side Complete this meal by serving a fruit compote as dessert.

1 cup chopped onions
1 cup shredded carrots
2 Tbsp. dried parsley flakes
1 tsp. dried tarragon
⅛ tsp. pepper
1 Tbsp. vegetable oil
2 8-oz. bottles clam juice
1¾ cup low-sodium tomato juice
½ cup water
⅓ cup small seashell pasta
1 lb. frozen white-flesh fish fillets, thawed

In saucepan, cook onions, carrots, parsley, tarragon, and pepper in oil, over medium heat. Stir often until onion is tender. Stir in clam and tomato juice, water, and pasta. Cover and simmer 10 minutes. Cut fish into 1-inch chunks. Add fish and cook for 5 to 10 minutes more.

Per serving
205 calories
49 mg cholesterol
347 mg sodium
0.58 gm saturated fat
3.7 gm fat

Exchanges per serving
1 bread
2 meat
1 vegetable

On the side Serve with cantaloupe melon slices as dessert for a nutritionally complete meal.

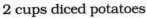
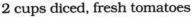

2 quarts water

1 tsp. salt

    2 cups chopped carrots

    2 cups diced potatoes

    2 cups diced, fresh tomatoes

    1 cup sliced green onions

    1 cup frozen lima beans

2 cups fresh green beans, cut into 1 inch pieces

1 cup frozen corn

½ cup instant rice

In 6-quart pan, combine everything except corn and rice. Cover and bring to a boil. Reduce heat and simmer for 30 minutes. Add corn and rice; simmer for 15 minutes. Serve.

Per serving

133 calories

0 mg cholesterol

237 mg sodium

0.07 gm saturated fat

0.36 gm fat

Exchanges per serving

1½ bread

1 vegetable

On the side Serve this hearty soup with a glass of milk and top off the meal with baked apples (one apple per person) for dessert and nutritional balance.

15 oz. very lean beef for stew, cubed
1½ quarts water
1 cup vegetable juice
1 cup chopped cabbage
½ cup chopped celery
¾ cup chopped green onions
2 oz. uncooked lentils
1 cup chopped carrots
1 cup peeled, chopped potatoes
1 tsp. minced garlic
½ cup sliced, fresh mushrooms
⅛ tsp. pepper
⅛ tsp. salt

On broiling pan, place beef and broil until browned on each side. Transfer beef to a 4-quart saucepan and add all of the ingredients. Bring to a boil. Reduce heat and simmer for 50 minutes.

Per serving
428 calories
103 mg cholesterol
287 mg sodium
6.1 gm saturated fat
16 gm fat

Exchanges per serving
1½ bread
3½ meat
1 vegetable

On the side Finish this meal with fresh fruit for nutritional balance.

1 lb. dried great northern beans, and water to cover
6 cups water
      3 carrots, sliced
      3 celery ribs, sliced
      2 medium onions, chopped
      2 garlic cloves, minced
      2 bay leaves
1 14½-oz. can tomatoes with liquid, cut up
1 tsp. dried basil
½ tsp. pepper
2 Tbsp. olive oil

Place the beans in a Dutch oven and cover with water; bring to a boil. Boil for 2 minutes. Remove from the heat; cover and let stand for 1 hour. Drain and rinse beans; return to Dutch oven. Add 6 cups water, carrots, celery, onions, garlic, bay leaves, tomatoes, basil and pepper; bring to a boil. Reduce heat; cover and simmer for 1½ hours or until the beans are tender. Discard bay leaves. Add oil and heat through.

Per serving
87 calories
0 mg cholesterol
166 mg sodium
0.3 gm saturated fat
2.6 gm fat

Exchanges per serving
2½ vegetable
½ fat

On the side Finish this meal off with a compote of your favorite fresh fruits.

1 fresh jalapeño chili pepper
1 Tbsp. vegetable oil
1 cup chopped onion
1 tsp. minced garlic
¾ tsp. cumin seed
6 cups low-sodium chicken broth
¾ cup rice
2 cups tomatoes, diced
1 10-oz. package frozen peas, thawed
¾ lb. tiny cooked shrimp

Cut jalapeño chili in half. In a 6-quart saucepan, combine oil, onion, garlic, cumin seed, and half of a jalapeño chili. Stir over medium heat until onion is tender. Add broth and rice; bring to a boil. Reduce heat and simmer for 30 minutes. Add tomatoes, peas, and shrimp. Remove and discard chili half.

Cut remaining chili into slices. Serve and sprinkle chili slices on top.

Per serving
200 calories
85 mg cholesterol
277 mg sodium
0.33 gm saturated fat
3.6 gm fat

Exchanges per serving
1 bread
1 meat
1 vegetable

On the side Chilled pears offer a refreshing taste as a dessert and to round out this complete meal.

½ lb. green split peas
½ tsp. minced garlic
½ tsp. ground cumin
¼ tsp. curry powder
½ tsp. ground ginger
6 cups water
1½ cup diced carrots
1 lb. boneless, skinless chicken breasts, cubed
¾ cup chopped onions
⅛ tsp. black pepper

Put peas, garlic, cumin, curry powder, and ginger in saucepan; add 6 cups water and slowly bring to a boil. Reduce heat and simmer for 40 minutes. Add carrots, chicken and onions; cook 15 to 20 minutes longer or until chicken is cooked through. Season with pepper.

Per serving
212 calories
71 mg cholesterol
76 mg sodium
2.3 gm saturated fat
4.2 gm fat

Exchanges per serving
1 bread
1 meat
1 vegetable

On the side Serve pears and apples with blueberries in a compote as a tasty follow-on to this spicy soup.

46   Avocado Tuna Salad in Pita Bread   *Serves 4*

1 6⅛-oz. can tuna in spring water, drained and flaked
1 cup chopped avocado, very ripe
¼ cup chopped tomatoes
¼ cup diced onions
1 tsp. lemon juice
1 tsp. dried parsley flakes
1 Tbsp. apple cider vinegar
¼ tsp. horseradish
2 6-inch whole-wheat pita bread rounds, halved

Combine ingredients in a bowl and blend thoroughly with a fork. Fill each pita half with ¼ of the tuna mixture.

Per serving
288 calories
10 mg cholesterol
73 mg sodium
1.3 gm saturated fat
5.6 gm fat

Exchanges per serving
1 bread
1 fat
2 meat

On the side Cantaloupe melon provides a refreshing and nutritious completer for this meal.

2 slices part-skim American cheese
1 tomato, thinly sliced
4 slices whole-wheat bread
nonstick cooking spray

Put cheese and tomato slices on two of the bread
slices; cover with remaining 2 slices of bread. Spray
skillet with nonstick cooking spray and toast each
side of sandwiches until golden brown.

Per serving
221 calories
15.9 mg cholesterol
493 mg sodium
2.8 gm saturated fat
7 gm fat

Exchanges per serving
2 bread
1 meat

On the side Cottage cheese (¼ cup per person), a fresh fruit, or a
glass of milk will complete this meal.

¼ cup plain low-fat yogurt
1½ Tbsp. light mayonnaise
1½ tsp. Dijon-style mustard
1 tsp. dried dillweed
⅛ tsp. black pepper
14¾ oz. can salmon in spring water, drained
½ cup finely chopped green pepper
¼ cup chopped onions
3 whole-wheat English muffins, halved and toasted

In a bowl, mix yogurt, mayonnaise, mustard, dillweed and pepper; blend well. In another bowl, mix salmon, green pepper and onion. Spoon over dressing, toss to coat. Refrigerate covered for 30 minutes. Divide evenly over muffins.

Per serving
220 calories
2.3 mg cholesterol
73 mg sodium
0.78 gm saturated fat
3.3 gm fat

Exchanges per serving
½ bread
1 fat
2 meat

On the side Honeydew melon adds a refreshing taste to this delicious sandwich. A glass of milk and a tossed salad nutritionally round out this meal.

Sauced Tuna Pita

1 6⅛-oz. can tuna
¼ cup shredded carrots
½ cup alfalfa sprouts
4 lettuce leaves
⅓ cup plain low-fat yogurt
½ cup chopped and peeled cucumber
2 Tbsp. sliced green onions
1 tsp. lemon juice
¾ tsp. dried dillweed
⅛ tsp. paprika
⅛ tsp. celery seed
2 6-inch pita bread rounds

In a bowl, combine all ingredients except lettuce leaves and alfalfa sprouts; toss gently. Line each pita half with lettuce leaves and alfalfa sprouts. Spoon tuna mixture evenly into each pita pocket half.

Per serving
169 calories
27 mg cholesterol
489 mg sodium
1.1 gm saturated fat
4.3 gm fat

Exchanges per serving
1 bread
1 meat
1 vegetable

On the side A cup of plain, low-fat yogurt adds 1½ milk and ½ fat exchanges or 144 calories to this meal. A piece of fruit makes the meal complete.

2 cups frozen, cooked small shrimp, thawed
½ cup frozen peas, thawed
½ cup chopped red pepper
⅓ cup low-cal creamy cucumber salad dressing
1 tsp. lime juice
1 tsp. dried thyme, crushed
2 cups shredded lettuce
4 6-inch pita bread rounds

Coarsely chop shrimp. In a mixing bowl, combine shrimp, peas, red pepper, salad dressing, lime juice, and thyme. Stir until combined. Add shredded lettuce to the shrimp mixture. Toss to mix. Cut pita bread in half. Spoon the shrimp mixture into pita pockets.

Per serving
190 calories
89 mg cholesterol
271 mg sodium
0.69 gm saturated fat
8.0 gm fat

Exchanges per serving
½ bread
1 fat
2 meat

On the side Cottage cheese, in ¼ cup servings, some crunchy vegetables, and a piece of fruit complete this meal.

Shrimp Stuffed Pitas

¾ cup cracked wheat
1 Tbsp. light mayonnaise
1 cup chopped cucumber
1 cup chopped tomatoes
2 tsp. Dijon-style mustard
3 tsp. red wine vinegar
½ cup lime juice
1 lb. cooked shrimp, peeled and deveined
6 6-inch whole-wheat pita bread pockets
6 leaves of lettuce

Prepare cracked wheat according to package directions; soak in water for at least one hour. Combine cracked wheat and all the other ingredients in mixing bowl; toss and blend. Split open the pitas, insert a lettuce leaf in each and stuff with salad mixture.

Per serving
225 calories
132 mg cholesterol
219 mg sodium
0.13 gm saturated fat
0.6 gm fat

Exchanges per serving
2 bread
½ fat
½ meat
1 vegetable

On the side Cottage cheese and fruit make this meal nutritionally balanced.

2 Tbsp. margarine

¾ cup sliced mushrooms

1 cup thinly sliced zucchini

1 tsp. minced garlic

⅛ tsp. pepper

½ cup shredded part-skim mozzarella cheese

¼ cup finely chopped tomato

½ cup alfalfa sprouts

1 Tbsp. grated Parmesan cheese

4 slices whole-wheat bread, toasted

In skillet, melt margarine. Sauté mushrooms, zucchini, garlic and pepper until crisp-tender; drain. Sprinkle ¼ cup shredded mozzarella cheese on 2 slices of toasted bread, arrange sautéed vegetables over cheese. Top with tomato and sprouts. Sprinkle with remaining mozzarella cheese and Parmesan cheese on top. Broil until cheeses melt. Top each with slices of bread. Cut in half diagonally.

Per serving
286 calories
11 mg cholesterol
109 mg sodium
2.3 gm saturated fat
6.83 gm fat

Exchanges per serving
2 bread
1 fat
½ meat
1 vegetable

On the side Adding some fresh tomatoes, arranged attractively on the plate around this sandwich, round out this meal.

1 8-oz. can pineapple slices in unsweetened juice
Nonstick cooking spray
8 oz. boneless skinless chicken breast, halved
2 tsp. pineapple juice
2 Tbsp. Dijon-style mustard
2 Tbsp. non-fat mayonnaise
1 Tbsp. soy sauce
2 tsp. honey
2 small whole-wheat rolls
¼ cup part-skim shredded Swiss cheese
2 slices onion

Drain pineapple and reserve two teaspoons of juice.
Spray skillet with cooking spray and brown the
chicken; cook until done. Combine in a bowl, 2 teaspoons pineapple juice, mustard, mayonnaise, soy
sauce and honey; spread rolls with sauce. Top each
sandwich with chicken, cheese, pineapple and onion.

Per Serving
414 calories
61 mg cholesterol
1,574 mg sodium
5.2 gm saturated fat
13.7 gm fat

Exchanges per serving
1 bread
1 fat
1 fruit
4 meat

On the side Cottage cheese (1/4 cup servings) or fresh crunchy
vegetables complete this meal.

1 Tbsp. margarine
4 cups sliced, fresh mushrooms
½ cup chopped onions
½ tsp. minced garlic
1 cup light sour cream
¼ tsp. dried thyme
½ tsp. lemon juice
⅛ tsp. pepper
16 slices whole-wheat bread

In skillet, melt margarine. Add mushrooms, onions and garlic, and cook until liquid evaporates, stirring frequently. Remove from heat. Stir in sour cream, thyme, lemon juice and pepper. Spread ¼ cup mushroom mixture on each of 8 bread slices. Top with remaining 8 slices of bread. Lightly spread margarine on outside of sandwiches. Heat skillet over medium heat and toast sandwiches on both sides.

Per serving
250 calories
12 mg cholesterol
317 mg sodium
0.5 gm saturated fat
4 gm fat

Exchanges per serving
2 bread
1 fat
1 vegetable

On the side Tomatoes and cucumbers on the side of this tasty sandwich provide a good accompaniment. A glass of skim milk completes the meal.

Tuna 'n Cheese Filled Pitas

1 9¼-oz. can tuna in spring water, drained
¾ cup part-skim shredded cheddar cheese
⅓ cup chopped celery
¼ cup chopped pecans
⅓ cup light sour cream
¼ cup light mayonnaise
2 6-inch pita bread rounds
1 cup shredded lettuce
½ cup alfalfa sprouts

In a mixing bowl, stir together tuna, shredded cheddar cheese, celery, pecans, sour cream, and mayonnaise. Cut pita bread in half to make a pocket. Line each pita half with lettuce and alfalfa sprouts. Spoon tuna mixture in each pocket half.

Per serving
298 calories
23 mg cholesterol
512 mg sodium
5.5 gm saturated fat
14.8 gm fat

Exchanges per serving
1 bread
1 fat
3 meat
1 vegetable

On the side Fresh pears, 1 per person, complete this meal and give it nutritional balance.

1 6⅛-oz. can tuna in spring water
⅓ cup low-fat plain yogurt
  ⅛ cup diced celery
  1½ tsp. Dijon-style mustard
  ¼ tsp. dried dillweed
  2 6-inch round pita breads, halved
  4 lettuce leaves
1 tomato, sliced

Combine tuna, yogurt, celery, mustard and dillweed.
Line bread halves with lettuce leaves and tomatoes.
Divide tuna mixture among bread halves. Serve
immediately.

Per serving
270 calories
1.8 mg cholesterol
220 mg sodium
0.5 gm saturated fat
0.8 gm fat

Exchanges per serving
1 bread
½ fat
3 meat

On the side Cottage cheese (¼ cup per person) and fresh peaches
complete this meal.

8 slices rye bread
4 Tbsp. low-calorie Thousand Island dressing
¾ lb. cooked fresh turkey tenderloin, sliced
2 cups sauerkraut
½ cup shredded part-skim Swiss cheese

Coat four slices rye bread evenly with Thousand
Island dressing. Top each with ¼ of turkey tenderloin,
½ cup sauerkraut and ¼ of the cheese; top with
second slice of rye bread. Grill until cheese melts and
turkey is heated through.

Per Serving
353 calories
57 mg cholesterol
1,438 mg sodium
2.6 gm saturated fat
10 gm fat

Exchanges per serving
2 bread
1 fat
4 meat
1 vegetable

On the side Cucumbers and tomatoes combine for a refreshing
addition to complete this meal.

58   Turkey Salad in a Pita

1 10-oz. can mandarin oranges in water
3 cups torn salad greens
⅓ cup low-calorie buttermilk salad dressing
½ tsp. dried tarragon
1 6-oz. pkg. sliced, cooked turkey breast
2 6-inch whole-wheat pita bread rounds, halved

Drain mandarin orange sections. In a bowl, mix mandarin oranges, salad greens, buttermilk dressing, and tarragon. Toss well to coat. Place 2 slices of turkey breast into each pita half. Divide salad mixture among the 4 pocket halves.

Per serving
184 calories
31 mg cholesterol
110 mg sodium
0.75 gm saturated fat
3.5 gm fat

Exchanges per serving
½ bread
½ fat
½ fruit
1½ meat

On the side Cottage cheese and some crunchy fresh vegetables make this a complete meal.

62 ∎ *One Year of Healthy, Hearty & Simple One-Dish Meals*

Pasta and Rice

6 oz. spaghetti
8 oz. package frozen cut asparagus, thawed

        ¾ tsp. basil
        ¾ tsp. thyme
        ½ tsp. onion powder
        1 cup chopped tomatoes
        ½ cup low-calorie Italian salad dressing
1 Tbsp. lemon juice

Cook spaghetti and asparagus separately according to package directions; drain. Toss spaghetti with basil, thyme, and onion powder. Add asparagus, tomatoes, salad dressing and lemon juice. Cover and chill in freezer for 10 to 15 minutes.

Per serving
179 calories
0 mg cholesterol
239 mg sodium
0.25 gm saturated fat
2.3 gm fat

Exchanges per serving
1½ bread
½ fat
1 vegetable

On the side Add a tossed salad and a fruit to make this meal nutritionally complete.

Cracked Wheat-Rice Pilaf

1⅓ cup water
½ cup cracked wheat
¼ cup long-grain rice
2 tsp. instant beef bouillon granules
¾ cup chopped carrots
½ cup chopped celery
¾ cup onions, chopped
⅛ tsp. salt
⅛ tsp. lemon pepper
½ tsp. celery seed

Combine all ingredients in a 2-quart saucepan. Bring to a boil. Reduce heat and simmer for 25 minutes.

Per serving
54 calories
0 mg cholesterol
539 mg sodium
0 gm saturated fat
0.5 gm fat

Exchanges per serving
½ bread
1 vegetable

On the side A glass of milk, a fresh vegetable salad and a piece of your favorite fruit for dessert round out this meal nutritionally.

4 oz. fettuccine

2 tsp. margarine

1½ cup sliced mushrooms

½ tsp. minced garlic

1 Tbsp. skim milk

⅓ cup grated Parmesan cheese

Cook fettuccine according to package directions. In a saucepan, heat margarine. Add mushrooms and garlic. Cook until tender. Add milk and Parmesan cheese. Toss gently until fettuccine is well coated.

Per serving
148 calories
28 mg cholesterol
51 mg sodium
0.57 gm saturated fat
4.6 gm fat

Exchanges per serving
1½ bread

On the side Add a salad of fresh, crunchy vegetables, a glass of milk and a fresh fruit to complete the meal.

8 oz. spinach fettuccine
2 tsp. margarine
¼ cup finely chopped onions
¾ tsp. minced garlic
2 tsp. cornstarch
1½ tsp. dried basil
1 tsp. instant chicken bouillon granules
⅔ cup skim milk
⅔ cup water
¼ cup grated Parmesan cheese

Cook pasta according to directions on package. In saucepan, melt margarine and cook onions and garlic until tender. Stir cornstarch, basil, bouillon granules; blend. Add milk and water. Cook and stir until thickened and bubbly. Toss with pasta. Sprinkle with cheese.

Per serving
231 calories
9.25 mg cholesterol
286 mg sodium
0.75 gm saturated fat
2.55 gm fat

Exchanges per serving
2 bread
1 fat

On the side A tossed salad, a glass of milk, and a piece of fresh fruit makes this meal nutritionally complete.

63   Mac-Tuna Casserole

1½ cup elbow macaroni
⅔ cup chopped carrots
½ cup chopped celery
½ cup chopped onions
1 can cream of celery soup
¾ cup skim milk
2 6⅛-oz. cans tuna in spring water
¾ cup frozen peas, thawed

Cook macaroni according to package directions; drain. Cook carrots, celery and onion in a small amount of water and steam the vegetables; drain.

Preheat oven to 375°F. In 2-quart casserole dish, combine macaroni, vegetables, soup and milk; blend. Fold in tuna and peas. Cover and bake for 30 minutes.

Per serving
290 calories
6.6 mg cholesterol
427 mg sodium
0.73 gm saturated fat
3.3 gm fat

Exchanges per serving
1½ bread
1 fat
2 meats

On the side Accompany with a tossed salad and finish the meal with fresh fruit.

4 oz. thin Italian noodles
½ cup green onions, chopped
1 Tbsp. coarsely grated ginger
2 tsp. soy sauce
2 tsp. red wine vinegar
½ tsp. sugar
1 tsp. sesame oil

Cook noodles according to directions on package. In large bowl, combine remaining ingredients; mix. Stir noodles into sauce.

Per serving
123 calories
0 mg cholesterol
1127 mg sodium
0.5 gm saturated fat
4.1 gm fat

Exchanges per serving
1½ bread

On the side Stir-fry your favorite vegetables and finish the meal off with fruit and yogurt for a nutritionally complete meal.

6 oz. vermicelli

3 tsp. sesame oil

½ tsp. Chinese five-spice powder (available in specialty stores or in Chinese markets)

2 Tbsp. soy sauce

1 tsp. sugar

¾ cup shredded cooked chicken

¼ cup green onions

1½ cups shredded red cabbage

1½ cups frozen peas, thawed

½ tsp. coriander

Cook pasta in boiling water; drain and rinse with cold water. Combine sesame oil, five-spice powder, soy sauce and sugar. Mix well. In large bowl, combine pasta with sesame oil mixture. Add chicken, green onions, cabbage, peas and coriander. Toss lightly.

Per serving
304 calories
35 mg cholesterol
543 mg sodium
2.75 gm saturated fat
11.5 gm fat

Exchanges per serving
2 bread
1 fat
1 meat

On the side Complete this meal nutritionally by adding a mélange of cooked peppers and a fruit compote for dessert.

1 Tbsp. olive oil
1 Tbsp. minced garlic
2½ cups sliced mushrooms
1½ cups sliced carrots
2½ cups water
1¼ cups low-sodium beef broth
1¼ cups uncooked small pasta shells
1 tsp. dried basil
1 tsp. lemon pepper
½ tsp. dried tarragon
½ tsp. oregano
¼ tsp. ground pepper
½ cup chopped onions
½ cup canned chickpeas, rinsed and drained
1 cup frozen peas
1 cup red kidney beans, drained

In saucepan, heat oil over medium heat. Add garlic and cook 1 minute. Add mushrooms and carrots; cook until tender. Add water and broth; bring to a boil. Stir in pasta and seasonings. Reduce heat and simmer 10 minutes. Add onions, chickpeas, peas and kidney beans. Simmer until vegetables are tender.

Per serving
168 calories
0 mg cholesterol
68.3 mg sodium
0.33 gm saturated fat
2.9 gm fat

Exchanges per serving
1½ bread
1 vegetable

On the side Fruit and yogurt make a perfect dessert.

2 small zucchinis, sliced
1 cup green beans, cut
1 cup shredded carrots
½ cup peas
⅔ cup olive oil
1 Tbsp. lemon juice
1 tsp. minced garlic
¾ tsp. oregano
¼ cup chopped green onions
1 lb. thin linguine

Steam zucchini, beans, carrots and peas over boiling water until peas are tender. Combine oil, lemon juice and garlic; mix well. Mix with steamed vegetables. Add oregano and green onions. Toss so that vegetables are well coated. Cook linguine according to package directions; drain. Place in serving dish. Pour vegetable mixture over linguine; toss to mix well and serve at once.

Per serving
399 calories
0 mg cholesterol
14 mg sodium
1.7 gm saturated fat
15 gm fat

Exchanges per serving
3 bread
2 fat
1 vegetable

On the side Mixed fruit compote with low-fat yogurt for dessert, and this meal is nutritionally complete.

Pasta Salad

Dressing:

3 Tbsp. vegetable oil
2 Tbsp. apple cider vinegar
½ tsp. ginger

Salad:

2 cups curly macaroni
¼ cup chopped green onions
1 mandarin orange, cut into pieces
¾ cup bean sprouts
1 6-oz. package frozen pea pods, thawed, rinsed, and
    drained

In small bowl, combine all dressing ingredients. Mix
well. Cook macaroni according to directions. Drain
and rinse with cold water. In large bowl, combine
macaroni, onion, orange, been sprouts, and pea pods.
Drizzle dressing over salad. Toss until combined.

Per serving
166 calories
0 mg cholesterol
68.66 mg sodium
0.83 gm saturated fat
7.5 gm fat

Exchanges per serving
1 bread
1 fat
1 fruit

On the side Serve this tasty salad with a glass of milk and your
meal is nutritionally complete.

1 Tbsp. olive oil
½ pound chicken breasts, boneless, skinless,
    cut into ¼-inch slices
1 medium onion, thinly sliced and
    separated into rings
2 cups mushrooms, thinly sliced
1 can artichoke hearts
14½ oz. can diced tomatoes
½ cup chicken broth
1 clove garlic, pressed
1 tsp. Italian seasoning
⅛ tsp. salt
⅛ tsp. pepper
½ lb. penne pasta, uncooked
½ cup fresh parsley, finely chopped

In a large pot, bring 3 quarts of water to a boil for the pasta. In a large nonstick skillet, heat the oil over high heat. Add the chicken and saute until cooked through and beginning to brown, about 3 minutes. Transfer to a plate. Turn heat to medium. Add onion and mushrooms to skillet and saute until onion is softened and mushrooms are lightly browned, about 5 minutes. Add artichoke hearts, undrained tomatoes, broth, garlic, Italian seasoning, salt, and pepper; mix gently. Cover and bring to a simmer; reduce heat and simmer 10 minutes. stir occasionally. Return chicken to skillet and mix gently. Cover and simmer until chicken is hot, about 2 minutes. Meanwhile, cook pasta according to package directions until tender but still firm. Drain and return to pot or to a large bowl. Add chicken mixture and parsley and toss.

Per serving

283 calories
60 mg cholesterol
548 mg sodium
1.2 gm saturated fat
6.5 gm fat

Exchanges per serving

1 meat
2 bread
2 vegetable
½ fat

On the side Add a glass of milk and fresh fruit to complete the meal.

2 cups finely chopped plum tomatoes

1½ Tbsp. light extra virgin olive oil, divided

1 tsp. dried basil leaves, divided

⅓ cup sweet onions, cut into slivers

2 Tbsp. sundried tomatoes, diced

2 cloves garlic, crushed

½ pound penne pasta

3 cups cauliflower florets

4 tsp. Parmesan cheese

Bring a large pot of water to a boil. Combine the tomatoes, 1 Tbsp. of oil, ½ tsp. basil, onion, sundried tomatoes, and garlic in a large bowl and stir to blend. Set aside. Stir the pasta into the boiling water and cook until slightly underdone, about 8 minutes. Stir in the cauliflower and cook, stirring occasionally, until cauliflower is tender and pasta is done. Drain. Add the penne pasta and cauliflower to the tomato mixture and toss to coat. Sprinkle with remaining olive oil and basil. Sprinkle cheese over each serving.

Per serving
310 calories
51 mg cholesterol
103 mg sodium
1.2 gm saturated fat
7 gm fat

Exchanges per serving
3 bread
2 vegetable
1 fat

On the side A glass of milk and a mixed fruit compote complete this meal.

Rice Casserole

1 cup chopped carrots
¾ cup chopped onions
2 cups sliced, fresh mushrooms
½ cup diced celery
¼ cup margarine
½ tsp. salt
½ tsp. paprika
½ tsp. garlic powder
½ cup green pepper
1 diced tomato
½ cup water
2 cups uncooked rice

Melt margarine in large skillet. Sauté all vegetables, except tomatoes, until tender. Add seasonings, tomato and water; bring to a boil. Stir in rice. Cover and simmer for 10 minutes or until rice is tender.

Per serving
235 calories
0 mg cholesterol
395 mg sodium
1.3 gm saturated fat
8 gm fat

Exchanges per serving
3 bread
1½ fat
1 vegetable

On the side A dessert of fruit with low-fat yogurt rounds out this meal nutritionally.

1½ Tbsp. margarine
½ cup chopped onion
¼ cup chopped celery
¾ cup rice
¾ cup vermicelli, broken up
1½ cups low-sodium chicken broth
¾ cup water
3 Tbsp. dry white wine
¼ tsp. salt
½ tsp. thyme
⅛ tsp. ground pepper
¼ cup dried parsley flakes

In skillet, melt margarine. Add onion and celery; cook until soft. Add rice and vermicelli and cook until lightly browned. Add remaining ingredients and bring to a boil. Reduce heat and simmer 30 to 40 minutes or until rice is tender.

Per serving
135 calories
0 mg cholesterol
173 mg sodium
0.5 gm saturated fat
3.2 gm fat

Exchanges per serving
1 bread
1 fat

On the side Serve this with a glass of nonfat milk and a compote of fresh fruit as dessert and your meal is complete.

1 Tbsp. vegetable oil
1½ tsp. minced garlic
⅓ cup chopped onions
6 cups diced tomatoes
2 Tbsp. tomato paste
⅛ tsp. pepper
½ tsp. oregano
¼ tsp. basil
1½ cups frozen peas, thawed
¾ lb. spaghetti
4 Tbsp. grated Parmesan cheese

Heat oil in a skillet over low heat and sauté garlic and onions for 2 minutes. Add tomatoes, tomato paste and cook over medium heat for 20 minutes. Add pepper, oregano, and basil. Stir in peas. Cook spaghetti according to package directions; drain. Toss with tomato-pea sauce. Serve with Parmesan cheese sprinkled on top.

Per serving
306 calories
8 mg cholesterol
127 mg sodium
1.5 gm saturated fat
7.15 gm fat

Exchanges per serving
2½ bread
1 fat
1 vegetable

On the side Serve with plain nonfat yogurt and fruit as dessert to complete this meal nutritionally.

Spinach Tortellini
with Tomato-Vegetable Sauce

Serves 4

1 Tbsp. olive oil
1 medium onion, diced
1 medium red bell pepper, diced
¾ cup carrots, thinly sliced
2 14½-oz. cans diced tomatoes
¾ tsp. dried oregano leaves
⅛ tsp. salt
⅛ tsp. pepper
14 oz. package spinach filled tortellini
4 Tbsp. Romano or Parmesan cheese

In a large nonstick skillet, heat oil over medium heat.
Add onion, bell pepper, and carrots. Saute until onion
is softened, about 5 minutes. Add undrained tomatoes, oregano, salt, and pepper; mix gently. Cover and
bring to a simmer. Reduce heat and simmer covered,
stirring occasionally, until vegetables are tender and
sauce is slightly thickened, about 25 minutes.
Meanwhile, cook the tortellini according to package
directions. Drain and return to a large bowl. Add
tomato sauce and toss. Serve with grated cheese.

Per serving
347 calories
20 mg cholesterol
1375 mg sodium
5.3 gm saturated fat
17 gm fat

Exchanges per serving
2 meat
3 vegetable
1 bread
2 fat

On the side Cantaloupe melon, a fresh pear, or a baked apple
complete the meal.

8 uncooked jumbo macaroni shells
3 Tbsp. low-calorie Italian dressing
¾ cup cottage cheese, part-skim
⅔ cup part-skim ricotta cheese
¼ cup chopped green onions
2 Tbsp. grated Parmesan cheese
1½ tsp. lemon juice
1 Tbsp. finely chopped red pepper
⅛ tsp. black pepper

Cook macaroni according to package directions. In a shallow glass bowl combine macaroni shells and Italian dressing; toss to coat. Cover and marinate in refrigerator for 1 hour. In a small bowl, combine remaining ingredients; mix. Remove shells from bowl, reserving dressing. Spoon ⅛ of cheese mixture into each shell. Drizzle with reserved dressing.

Per serving
262 calories
36 mg cholesterol
512 mg sodium
6.15 gm saturated fat
11.35 gm fat

Exchanges per serving
2 bread
2 fat
1 meat

On the side Serve with a fresh tomato and vegetable salad and a fruit for dessert to complete this meal nutritionally.

2 Tbsp. olive oil
1 cup finely grated onion
2 tsp. minced garlic
3 cups chopped tomatoes
⅛ tsp. salt
⅛ tsp. pepper
1 lb. spaghetti
2½ cups grated zucchini
2 Tbsp. fresh basil
1 Tbsp. margarine
¼ cup grated Parmesan cheese

In a skillet, heat oil. Add onions and garlic; cook until soft and golden. Add tomatoes, salt and pepper. Prepare spaghetti according to package directions. Just before spaghetti is ready, add zucchini and basil to the tomato mixture and simmer for 5 minutes. Drain spaghetti and toss with margarine. Top spaghetti with vegetable mixture. Serve with Parmesan cheese.

Per serving
261 calories
5 mg cholesterol
111 mg sodium
1.7 gm saturated fat
9.3 gm fat

Exchanges per serving
2½ bread
1½ fat
2 vegetable

On the side Start the meal with an antipasto of low-fat, thinly sliced meats of your choice. Finish off with a refreshing blend of mixed fruits.

1 can cream of celery soup
1 cup skim milk
1 cup water
½ tsp. dillweed
½ tsp. celery seed
¼ cup chopped onions
3 cups uncooked noodles
1 cup frozen peas
1 6⅛-oz. can tuna in spring water

In large skillet, combine soup, milk, water, dillweed, celery seed and onions. Bring to a boil. Add noodles and bring to a second boil. Reduce heat and simmer until noodles are tender. Stir in peas and tuna. Cook covered an additional 15 minutes.

Per serving
352 calories
13.7 mg cholesterol
387 mg sodium
0.7 gm saturated fat
2.8 gm fat

Exchanges per serving
2½ bread
1 fat
1 meat

On the side This easy one-dish meal needs only a tossed salad and a fruit to be a complete meal nutritionally.

14½ oz. can diced tomatoes
¼ cup fresh basil, minced
3 Tbsp. scallions, thinly sliced
1 Tbsp. extra virgin olive oil
1 clove garlic, minced
⅛ tsp. salt
⅛ tsp. pepper
½ lb. vegetable linguine, uncooked

In a large bowl, gently stir together undrained tomatoes, basil, scallions, oil, garlic, salt, and pepper. In a large pot, bring 3 quarts of water to boil. Add pasta and cook according to package directions, without adding salt, until tender but firm. Drain and return to pot or add to sauce. Toss to combine. (Prepare the sauce before you boil the pasta water to let the flavors develop.)

Per serving
249 calories
0 mg cholesterol
160 mg sodium
0.6 gm saturated fat
4 gm fat

Exchanges per serving
3 bread
1 vegetable
½ fat

On the side Complete this meal by serving fresh fruit for dessert.

8 oz. uncooked spaghetti
4 Tbsp. margarine
½ cup chopped green peppers
½ cup chopped onion
1 cup fresh sliced mushrooms
1½ Tbsp. flour
1½ cup skim milk
¼ tsp. salt
⅛ tsp. nutmeg
2½ cups hot cooked vegetables, any kind
½ cup grated Parmesan cheese

Cook spaghetti according to package directions; drain and rinse with hot water. In saucepan, melt margarine and sauté green pepper, onions and mushrooms until tender. Add flour, milk, salt and nutmeg. Blend and bring to a boil over medium heat. Remove and stir in cooked vegetables. Toss spaghetti and sauce in large bowl. Sprinkle with Parmesan cheese.

Per serving
318 calories
12.5 mg cholesterol
357 mg sodium
3 gm saturated fat
11.5 gm fat

Exchanges per serving
2 bread
2 fat
½ skim milk
1 vegetable

On the side Top this meal off with your favorite fruit and you have a nutritionally complete meal.

4 large red bell peppers, roasted
2 Tbsp. Italian parsley leaves
½ cup fresh basil leaves
1 clove garlic, peeled and quartered
5 tsp. light extra virgin olive oil
¼ tsp. salt
¼ tsp. pepper
1¼ cup chicken broth, defatted, low sodium, divided
1 lb. vermicelli
6 tsp. grated Parmesan cheese

In a food processor, place roasted peppers, parsley, basil, garlic, olive oil, salt, pepper, and 1 cup broth. Process until pureed. Cook pasta in 6 quarts boiling water until done. Transfer pasta to a bowl and toss with pepper puree. Add remaining broth and toss again. Sprinkle each serving with Parmesan cheese.

Per serving
414 calories
2 mg cholesterol
689 mg sodium
1 gm saturated fat
5 gm fat

Exchanges per serving
5 bread
1 vegetable
1 fat

On the side Add a serving fresh fruit for dessert to complete the meal.

Zucchini Lasagna

9 lasagna noodles
1 cup part-skim ricotta cheese
½ cup grated Parmesan cheese
1 Tbsp. dried parsley flakes
⅛ tsp. ground pepper
4 cups tomato sauce (low sodium)
½ cup chopped onion
1 tsp. oregano
1 tsp. basil
2½ cups chopped zucchini
1 cup part-skim shredded mozzarella cheese

Heat oven to 400°F. Cook noodles as directed on package; drain. In bowl, combine ricotta cheese, Parmesan cheese, parsley and ground pepper. Set aside. In saucepan, add tomato sauce, onions, oregano and basil. Bring to a boil stirring occasionally. Cover and simmer for 10 minutes. In a 13 x 9-inch pan, layer ¼ of the tomato sauce mixture, 3 lasagna noodles, ⅓ of the cheese mixture and ⅓ of the chopped zucchini. Repeat layers two more times. Spoon remaining sauce over top; sprinkle with mozzarella cheese. Bake for 35 to 40 minutes.

Per serving
190 calories
13.7 mg cholesterol
140.6 mg sodium
2.5 gm saturated fat
4.4 gm fat

Exchanges per serving
1 bread
½ fat
1 meat
1 vegetable

On the side Complete the meal with your favorite fresh fruit to round it out nutritionally.

4 oz. noodles
½ cup chopped celery
1 Tbsp. margarine
1 10¾ oz. can cream of chicken soup
½ cup plain low-fat yogurt
1½ Tbsp. skim milk
½ tsp. Worcestershire sauce
3 Tbsp. wheat germ

Preheat oven to 350°F. Cook noodles according to package directions; drain. In saucepan, cook celery in margarine. Stir in soup, yogurt, milk, and Worcestershire sauce. Fold in noodles. Place in casserole dish. Sprinkle wheat germ on top. Bake for 35 minutes.

Per serving
135 calories
9.1 mg cholesterol
445 mg sodium
1.3 gm saturated fat
6 gm fat

Exchanges per serving
1½ bread
1 fat

On the side Pick your favorite ingredients for a crunchy tossed salad, and enjoy fruit and low-fat plain yogurt for dessert and the meal is nutritionally complete.

Vegetables & Legumes

1 Tbsp. vegetable oil
1½ cup chopped red pepper
¼ cup chopped green onion
1 Tbsp. chili powder
1 Tbsp. ground cumin
¾ tsp. garlic powder
2 15-oz. cans black beans
⅓ cup ketchup
¼ cup low-fat yogurt
1 cup part-skim cheddar cheese, shredded

In saucepan, heat oil. Add red peppers and green onions; sauté. Stir in chili powder, cumin and garlic powder; sauté for 30 seconds. Add black beans with their liquid and simmer for 20 to 25 minutes. Add ketchup and simmer for 10 more minutes. Stir in yogurt and simmer until heated. Sprinkle with cheddar cheese. Simmer until cheese melts.

Per serving
255 calories
18.7 mg cholesterol
311 mg sodium
4.4 gm saturated fat
9.3 gm fat

Exchanges per serving
1½ bread
1 fat
1 meat
1 vegetable

On the side Serve this with a glass of milk and a fresh fruit for dessert and the meal is nutritionally complete.

Cabbage with Noodles

Serves 6 **84**

1 cup dry noodles
2½ cups finely chopped cabbage
1 Tbsp. margarine
¾ tsp. caraway seeds
½ tsp. onion powder

Cook noodles according to package directions,
omitting salt. In skillet, heat margarine. Add
cabbage and stir-fry until cabbage is tender. Add
drained noodles, caraway seed and onion powder. Stir
together and heat through.

Per serving
104 calories
0 mg cholesterol
30.6 mg sodium
0.3 mg saturated fat
1.9 gm fat

Exchanges per serving
1 bread
1 vegetable

On the side Add a glass of milk and a baked apple and the meal
is complete nutritionally.

2 cups chopped celery
1 cup chopped onion
   1 Tbsp. minced garlic
   1 cup chopped green pepper
   ½ cup chopped red pepper
   1 cup chopped cucumber
   1 cup low-sodium chicken broth
1 eggplant, peeled and cut into cubes
1 16-oz. can low-sodium tomato purée
⅛ tsp. cayenne
1½ Tbsp. soy sauce
1 cup whole-wheat bread crumbs

This is a LOW FAT DISH

Preheat oven to 350°F. Sauté celery, onion, garlic, green and red pepper, and cucumber in broth until thoroughly cooked. Add the eggplant, tomato purée, cayenne and soy sauce. Place mixture in a casserole dish and cover with bread crumbs. Cover and bake for 30 minutes. Uncover and bake an additional 10 to 15 minutes.

Per serving
120 calories
0 mg cholesterol
63 mg sodium
0.16 gm saturated fat
0.9 gm fat

Exchanges per serving
½ bread
2 vegetable

On the side Add a glass of low-fat milk and a fresh pear for a nutritionally complete meal.

1 large eggplant, sliced
1 Tbsp. vegetable oil
1 16-oz. jar marinara sauce
1 Tbsp. dried parsley flakes, crushed
4 Tbsp. grated Parmesan cheese
⅛ tsp. pepper
⅛ tsp. salt
½ cup shredded part-skim mozzarella cheese

Preheat oven to 375°F. Brush eggplant with oil and place on a nonstick baking sheet; broil until brown on both sides. In a 9-inch baking dish, place ¼ cup of marinara sauce on bottom. Add a layer of eggplant slices, top with some sauce, parsley, and 2 tablespoons Parmesan cheese. Repeat with a second layer. Season with salt and pepper. Sprinkle with mozzarella cheese. Bake for 20 minutes.

Per serving
160 calories
21.5 mg cholesterol
974 mg sodium
4.35 gm saturated fat
10.2 gm fat

Exchanges per serving
½ fat
1 meat
2 vegetable

On the side Serve with new potatoes, a glass of milk, and a fresh fruit for a nutritionally balanced meal.

1 lb. eggplant
1 medium tomato, chopped
⅔ cup low-sodium vegetable juice
1 tsp. dried basil
½ tsp. oregano
1 tsp. minced garlic
¾ cup part-skim mozzarella cheese, shredded
½ tsp. black pepper

Heat oven to 350°F. Peel and slice eggplant. Layer in 8-inch baking dish; top with tomatoes. In bowl, combine remaining ingredients except cheese; mix. Pour over eggplant and tomatoes. Sprinkle with cheese. Bake 35 to 40 minutes.

Per serving
81 calories
14 mg. cholesterol
81 mg sodium
2.32 gm saturated fat
3.75 gm fat

Exchanges per serving
½ meat
1 vegetable

On the side A glass of milk, a slice of your favorite bread, and fresh fruit for dessert makes this meal nutritionally complete.

Eggplant Parmigiana

1 lb lean ground beef
⅛ tsp. salt
⅛ tsp. pepper
½ cup chopped onions
¼ tsp. oregano
1 6-oz. can low-sodium tomato paste
1⅔ cup water
1 medium eggplant
¼ cup grated part-skim mozzarella cheese

Preheat oven to 350°F. In a skillet, brown beef; drain fat. Add salt, pepper, onions, and oregano. Add tomato paste and stir in water. Simmer for 15 minutes. Peel eggplant and slice. Spoon a thin layer of meat sauce into a baking dish. Arrange a single layer of eggplant slices over sauce. Repeat. Sprinkle with mozzarella cheese. Bake for 30 minutes.

Per serving
258 calories
68 mg cholesterol
142 mg sodium
5.8 gm saturated fat
13.9 gm fat

Exchanges per serving
3 meat
1 vegetable

On the side A serving of white rice, a glass of milk, and a cup of melon balls, or your favorite fresh fruit for dessert, completes this meal nutritionally.

1½ cup dried lentils, washed and drained
1½ cup finely chopped onion
    1 Tbsp. minced garlic
    1 tsp. ground cumin
    ½ cup fresh tomatoes, diced
    ¼ tsp. black pepper
    1 tsp. red wine vinegar

Simmer lentils in water for 1 hour or until they are
tender; drain. In large saucepan, cook onions and garlic with ¼ cup water until onions are soft. Add cumin,
tomatoes, and pepper. Cook a few minutes. Add lentils
and heat through. Stir in vinegar. Serve.

Per serving
90 calories
0 mg cholesterol
8 mg sodium
0 gm saturated fat
0 gm fat

Exchanges per serving
1 bread

On the side A glass of milk and a fresh fruit of your choice round
out this meal.

Pan Vegetable Pizza

2½ cups whole wheat flour
1 package active dry yeast
1 tsp. salt
¾ cup warm water
2 Tbsp. olive oil, divided
2½ cups sliced mushrooms
¼ cup chopped onions
1 small green pepper, chopped
1 8-oz. can low-sodium tomato sauce
½ cup chopped tomato
2 cups shredded part-skim mozzarella cheese
1 Tbsp. Parmesan cheese, grated

For crust, mix: 1½ cups flour, yeast and salt. Stir in water and 1 tablespoon oil. With mixer on low speed, beat until flour is just moistened. Knead with enough remaining flour to make a moderately stiff dough that is smooth and elastic. Cover with towel and set aside to rise, about 30 to 45 minutes. Preheat oven to 375°F. In a skillet, heat remaining oil. Add mushrooms, onions, green peppers, and cook until tender. Form dough to fit a 13 x 9 x 2-inch pan (spray pan with nonstick spray). Spread tomato sauce over dough. Sprinkle mushrooms, onions, peppers, and tomatoes evenly over dough. Sprinkle with cheeses. Bake for 20 to 25 minutes.

Per serving
240 calories
28.8 mg cholesterol
504 mg sodium
5.6 gm saturated fat
12 gm fat

Exchanges per serving
1 bread
1 fat
1 meat
2 vegetable

On the side Serve with a glass of milk and top off the meal with a fresh fruit of your choice.

1 head cabbage, shredded
3 Granny Smith apples, peeled, cored, and sliced
    ½ tsp. ground clove
    ⅛ tsp. fennel seed
    ¼ cup cider vinegar
    ½ cup apple juice concentrate

This is a **LOW FAT DISH**

Combine all ingredients in a skillet and cook over medium heat for 40 to 45 minutes.

Per serving
85 calories
0 mg cholesterol
11 mg sodium
0 gm saturated fat
0.52 gm fat

Exchanges per serving
1 fruit
1 vegetable

On the side Complete this meal nutritionally by serving a glass of milk and a slice of your favorite fresh bread.

6 red peppers, seeded and cored
1 Tbsp. olive oil
¾ cup chopped onions
1½ cup sliced mushrooms
3 cups cooked rice
1 Tbsp. dried parsley flakes, crushed
½ tsp. dried basil
2 cups vegetable juice
1 Tbsp. ketchup

Preheat oven to 350°F. Place peppers in a baking pan. In a skillet, heat oil and sauté onion. Add mushrooms and cook until soft. Add rice, parsley, basil; mix. Add vegetable juice and ketchup; mix. Stuff the pepper with the mixture. Bake for 50 to 60 minutes until tender.

Per serving
202 calories
0 mg cholesterol
325 mg sodium
0.4 gm saturated fat
2.9 gm fat

Exchanges per serving
2 bread
½ fat
2 vegetable

On the side Enjoy a glass of nonfat milk and choose your favorite fresh fruit for dessert and your meal is nutritionally complete.

1½ quarts water
2 green peppers, halved and seeded
¼ lb. lean ground beef
½ cup chopped onions
⅛ tsp. ground pepper
½ cup low-sodium tomato sauce
1 tsp. oregano
1 tsp. basil
1 tsp. garlic
1 cup part-skim shredded mozzarella cheese

Heat oven to 350°F. In saucepan, bring water to a boil. Put green peppers in water and boil for 3 to 4 minutes; drain.

In skillet, brown beef; drain off fat. Add onions, ground pepper, tomato sauce, oregano, basil and garlic. Stir and heat thoroughly. Place green pepper halves in baking dish. Fill with meat mixture. Sprinkle with mozzarella cheese. Bake for 20 minutes.

Per serving
161 calories
37 mg cholesterol
155 mg sodium
4 gm saturated fat
9 gm fat

Exchanges per serving
2 meat
1 vegetable

On the side A glass of milk, a slice of your favorite bread, and fresh fruit for dessert make this a nutritionally complete meal.

Squash and Spinach Casserole

Serves 4 **94**

2 eggs
4 cups cooked spaghetti squash
1 10-oz. package frozen chopped spinach
1½ cup sliced, fresh mushrooms
¼ cup finely chopped red pepper
⅓ cup bean sprouts
1 packet low-calorie chicken gravy mix, prepared
    according to package directions
¾ cup part-skim shredded mozzarella cheese

Preheat oven to 375°F. In mixing bowl, beat eggs; add squash, mix well. In a one-quart casserole dish, spread squash mixture evenly in dish. Bake for 15 to 20 minutes. In mixing bowl, combine remaining ingredients, except cheese; blend well. Spread spinach mixture over squash. Sprinkle with cheese. Bake until cheese is melted and browned, 20 to 25 minutes.

Per serving
249 calories
306 mg cholesterol
539 mg sodium
5.6 gm saturated fat
11.65 gm fat

Exchanges per serving
2 bread
½ meat
1 vegetable

On the side Serve this casserole with a glass of nonfat milk and a compote of fresh fruits for dessert for a nutritionally balanced meal.

2 green onions, finely chopped
1 Tbsp. fresh ginger root
1 clove garlic, finely sliced
4 oz. green beans
5 oz. baby corn
1 zucchini
½ lb. baby carrots
2 Tbsp. vegetable oil
1½ Tbsp. soy bean sauce
3 Tbsp. soy sauce
1 Tbsp. sesame oil
½ lb. Chinese egg noodles, cooked
1 Tbsp. sesame seeds

Prepare the green onions, ginger, and garlic. Trim all of
the vegetables and slice them finely and diagonally.
Heat the vegetable oil in a wok and add all the prepared
vegetables plus the green onions, ginger and garlic.
Stir-fry briskly together for 4 to 5 minutes. Add the soy
bean sauce and soy sauce and stir fry 2 minutes
longer, then cover and cook until all the vegetables are
tender but slightly crisp. Add the sesame oil. Add the
cooked noodles and toss to mix with the vegetables.
Sprinkle with the sesame seeds and serve immediately.

Per serving
231 calories
18 mg cholesterol
1198 mg sodium
1.6 gm saturated fat
12.3 gm fat

Exchanges per serving
2 vegetable
2 ½ fat
1 bread

On the side Complete this meal by serving a glass of milk and
fresh fruit.

Stuffed Green Peppers

1 Tbsp. vegetable oil
½ cup chopped onion
½ cup chopped carrots
½ cup chopped celery
1 Tbsp. minced garlic
½ cup water
2 cups low-sodium beef broth
½ tsp. dried oregano
¼ tsp. dried basil
⅛ tsp. ground pepper
1 16-oz. can low-sodium stewed tomatoes
½ cup uncooked rice
6 large green peppers
⅓ cup shredded part-skim mozzarella cheese

Preheat oven to 350°F. In a skillet, heat oil. Add
onions, carrots, celery and garlic; cook until
vegetables are tender-crisp. Add water, beef broth,
oregano, basil and pepper; bring to a boil. Add
undrained tomatoes and uncooked rice; reduce heat
and simmer until rice is tender. Cut tops from green
peppers; clean and discard seeds. Cook whole
peppers in boiling water for 5 minutes. Drain and
stuff with rice mixture. Top with cheese. Bake for 30
to 35 minutes.

Per serving
117 calories
7.1 mg cholesterol
168 mg sodium
1.58 gm saturated fat
4.85 gm fat

On the side Serve these tasty peppers with a glass of cold nonfat
milk and top off the meal with some fresh fruit.

½ cup chopped green pepper
2 large tomatoes
    ½ cup sliced green onions
    ¼ cup bran cereal, uncooked

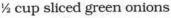
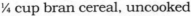

    1 egg
    ⅛ tsp. dried basil
    ⅛ tsp. oregano
½ Tbsp. dried parsley flakes

Heat oven to 350°F. Simmer green pepper in sauce-pan of water on stove for about 2 minutes. Slice each tomato in half. Scoop out pulp; chop pulp. In a bowl, mix tomato pulp, green pepper and remaining ingredients except parsley. Place tomato halves in baking dish. Fill each half with green pepper mixture. Sprinkle with parsley. Bake for 30 minutes.

Per serving
49 calories
53 mg cholesterol
50 mg sodium
0.5 gm saturated fat
1.7 gm fat

Exchanges per serving
1 vegetable

On the side White rice on the side of this colorful main dish adds a bread course. A glass of milk and a fruit for dessert make the meal nutritionally complete.

Tuna-Stuffed Tomato

Serves 4 **98**

4 tomatoes (6 oz. each)
¼ cup diced onions
¼ cup diced celery
2 tsp. Worcestershire sauce
⅛ tsp. pepper
⅛ tsp. pepper
2 6⅛-oz. cans tuna in spring water, drained
5 Tbsp. herb-seasoned bread crumbs

Preheat oven to 350°F. Cut slice off top of tomatoes; save slice. Remove and discard core. Scoop out pulp. Chop pulp and transfer to skillet. Add onion, celery, Worcestershire sauce, and pepper; cook over medium heat until all liquid evaporates. Remove from heat and add tuna and bread crumbs; mix well. Spoon tuna mixture into tomato shell and top with reserved tomato slices. Bake for 15 to 20 minutes.

Per serving
250 calories
10 mg cholesterol
194 mg sodium
0.25 gm saturated fat
1.3 gm fat

Exchanges per serving
½ bread
2 meat
1 vegetable

On the side White rice is an appropriate accompaniment to this main dish. Fruit and milk complete the meal nutritionally.

Vegetables & Legumes ■ 105

3 Tbsp. vegetable oil
¾ cup diced onion
1 tsp. minced garlic
2 cups sliced potatoes
½ cup sliced carrots
1 cup chopped zucchini
1 cup low-sodium tomato sauce
1½ tsp. oregano
1½ tsp. basil
¾ tsp. cumin
⅛ tsp. pepper

In a skillet, heat oil. Add onions and garlic; sauté. Add the remaining ingredients; mix. Simmer, covered, until potatoes are tender

Per serving
242 calories
0 mg cholesterol
75 mg sodium
1.25 gm saturated fat
10 gm fat

Exchanges per serving
2 bread
1 fat
1 vegetable

On the side A glass of cold, nonfat milk and a fresh fruit for dessert make this meal nutritionally complete.

Vegetable Medley

1 cup cauliflower
1 cup broccoli
1 cup chopped carrots
1 cup chopped onions
1 cup green peppers
1 cup green beans
1 Tbsp. cornstarch
⅛ tsp. salt
¾ cup skim milk
4 Tbsp. margarine
2 Tbsp. dried dillweed
2 Tbsp. dried parsley flakes
1 Tbsp. lemon juice
¾ cup whole wheat bread crumbs
2 Tbsp. Parmesan cheese, grated

Heat oven to 350°F. Steam all vegetables until crisp-
tender. In saucepan, combine cornstarch and salt.
Add milk and 2 tablespoons margarine; bring to a
boil. Remove from heat. Stir in dillweed, parsley and
lemon juice. Toss with vegetables; put into baking
dish. In small bowl combine bread crumbs, Parmesan
cheese and 2 tablespoons melted margarine; mix.
Sprinkle bread crumb mixture over vegetables. Bake
20 minutes.

Per serving
128 calories
1 mg cholesterol
266 mg sodium
2 gm saturated fat
8 gm fat

Exchanges per serving
½ bread
1 fat
2 vegetables

On the side A serving of brown rice, a glass of milk, and fruit
compote for dessert make this meal complete.

7 egg whites
½ cup chopped carrots
    ½ cup green beans, cut

    ½ cup chopped green pepper
    ½ cup corn
    ¼ cup chopped onion
    1 tsp. celery seed
1 tsp. dillweed
1 tsp. dry mustard
½ cup skim milk
½ cup light mayonnaise
½ cup flour
⅛ tsp. black pepper
⅛ tsp. salt

Heat oven to 325°F. Beat egg whites until stiff. In soufflé dish, mix all other ingredients. Fold egg whites into vegetable mixture. Bake 40 minutes.

Per serving
70 calories
2.6 mg cholesterol
110 mg sodium
0.37 gm saturated fat
2.1 gm fat

Exchanges per serving
1 fat
1 vegetable

On the side Serve this tasty soufflé with a slice of your favorite bread, a glass of cold nonfat milk, and top off the meal with a blend of melon balls and fresh berries.

Vegetarian Chili

2 cups red kidney beans
2 cups fresh chopped tomatoes
1¼ cups chopped onion
1 cup chopped green pepper
1 Tbsp. minced garlic
1 6-oz. can low-sodium tomato paste
¾ cup water
1 Tbsp. chili powder
1 Tbsp. soy sauce
½ tsp. ground cumin
½ tsp. ground pepper
½ tsp. oregano
4 cups brown rice, cooked

Drain kidney beans and set aside. In saucepan add tomatoes, onions, green peppers, garlic, tomato paste, water, chili powder, soy sauce, cumin, black pepper and oregano. Bring to a boil. Reduce heat; cover and simmer, stirring occasionally until mixture is thick and well blended, about 1½ to 2 hours. Stir in kidney beans and cook 15 minutes. Serve on brown rice.

Per serving
196 calories
0 mg cholesterol
531 mg sodium
0 gm saturated fat
2.4 gm fat

Exchanges per serving
2 bread
1 vegetable

On the side A glass of nonfat milk and a fresh chilled pear complete this meal nutritionally.

103 Zucchini Bake

Serves 6

6 small zucchini
1 cup herb-seasoned bread crumbs
¼ cup chopped onions
1 tsp. dried parsley flakes
⅛ tsp. salt
⅛ tsp. pepper
½ tsp. paprika
2 Tbsp. vegetable oil

Preheat oven to 350°F. Scrub zucchini and remove stem ends. Cook zucchini in boiling water for 4 minutes. Slice each zucchini lengthwise and hollow out the centers. Chop the pulp and in a bowl, mix pulp, ¼ cup bread crumbs, onions, parsley, salt, pepper and paprika. Fill the zucchini with the mixture. Mix ¾ cup bread crumbs and vegetable oil. Place zucchini in baking dish and sprinkle bread crumb mixture over zucchini. Bake 30 minutes.

Per serving
92 calories
0 mg cholesterol
64 mg sodium
0.5 gm saturated fat
4.6 gm fat

Exchanges per serving
½ bread
1 vegetable

On the side A serving of new potatoes, a glass of milk, and a baked apple complete this meal nutritionally.

110 ■ *One Year of Healthy, Hearty & Simple One-Dish Meals*

Zucchini and Citrus Salad

3 medium zucchinis
1 lemon, thinly sliced
1 lime, thinly sliced
2 Tbsp. mint leaves
1½ Tbsp. sugar
¼ cup vegetable oil
4 Tbsp. orange juice
1½ tsp. orange peel, grated

Cut zucchini into 2-inch long, ¼ inch thick sticks. In a
5-quart saucepan, cook zucchini in boiling water for 3
to 4 minutes. In a large bowl, combine lemon, lime,
mint, sugar, oil, orange juice, and orange peel.
Combine zucchini with dressing; toss and serve.

Per serving
114 calories
0 mg cholesterol
35 mg sodium
1.2 gm saturated fat
9.61 gm fat

Exchanges per serving
1 fat
½ fruit
1 vegetable

On the side Garnish the plates with sections of fresh oranges,
serve with your favorite bread and a glass of milk for a
nutritionally balanced meal.

½ Tbsp. vegetable oil
¼ cup chopped onions
1½ cups shredded zucchini
½ cup bran cereal, uncooked
¼ cup part-skim mozzarella cheese, shredded
1 egg
¼ tsp. basil
¼ tsp. oregano
⅛ tsp. black pepper
½ cup low-sodium tomato sauce

Heat oven to 375°F. In a skillet, heat oil; sauté onions until tender. In a bowl, mix onions, zucchini, and remaining ingredients except tomato sauce; mix well. Pour into 8-inch baking dish. Spread tomato sauce evenly over top. Bake 30 minutes.

Per serving
83 calories
48 mg cholesterol
74 mg sodium
1.45 gm saturated fat
3.91 gm fat

Exchanges per serving
½ meat
1 vegetable

On the side Serve with a slice of bread, a glass of milk, and some honeydew melon (or fruit of your choice) for a nutritionally balanced, low-calorie meal.

Zucchini Stir-Fry

2 Tbsp. vegetable oil
2 tsp. minced garlic
2 med. zucchinis, sliced
¼ cup chopped red pepper
2 cups pea pods
2 cups bean sprouts, rinsed
½ tsp. salt

In a skillet, heat oil on high. Stir-fry garlic until golden. Add zucchini, red pepper, pea pods; stir-fry 1 minute. Add bean sprouts and salt; stir-fry until crisp-tender.

Per serving
85 calories
0 mg cholesterol
187 mg sodium
0.6 gm saturated fat
4.8 gm fat

Exchanges per serving
1 fat
1 vegetable

On the side Brown rice, milk, and fresh fruit round out this meal nutritionally.

Beef
& Veal

12 oz. flank steak

1 tsp. sherry

2 Tbsp. ketchup

1 tsp. minced garlic

1 tsp. minced onion

1 Tbsp. hoisin sauce*

1 tsp. soy sauce

1 tsp. Worcestershire sauce

Cut steak into strips 2 inches wide. Combine remaining ingredients in bowl and add steak, stirring to coat. Place steak on broiling pan and broil to desired doneness. Brush frequently with marinade.

* Available in the Oriental food section of most grocery stores.

Per serving
300 calories
77 mg cholesterol
724 mg sodium
4.43 gm saturated fat
7.6 gm fat

Exchanges per serving
4 meat

On the side Cook up some fresh corn on the cob, pour a glass of cold nonfat milk, and end the meal with a tasty mixture of fresh fruits for nutritional balance.

Beef and Cabbage Casserole

Serves 6 **108**

1 lb. extra lean ground beef
⅓ cup diced onions
¼ tsp. garlic powder
3 cups shredded cabbage
1 cup sliced carrots
½ cup low-sodium beef broth
¼ tsp. pepper
½ tsp. caraway seed

Preheat oven to 450°F. Combine beef, onion, and garlic powder in a casserole dish. Bake for 15 minutes. Stir occasionally to break up meat. Drain fat. Turn oven down to 350°F and add cabbage, carrots, broth, pepper, and caraway seed. Blend well. Cover and bake 60 minutes.

Per serving
225 calories
111 mg cholesterol
303 mg sodium
4.0 gm saturated fat
10.3 gm fat

Exchanges per serving
2½ meat
1 vegetable

On the side Serve with a slice of your favorite fresh bread or a small dinner roll, a glass of milk, and end with baked apples for a meal that's delicious and nutritionally complete.

Beef & Veal ■ 117

1 lb. lean beef stew meat, cut into cubes
1 cup low-sodium beef broth
½ cup chopped onion
¼ cup chopped celery
⅛ tsp. pepper
¼ cup flour
½ cup whole-wheat bread crumbs
4 cups cooked rice

Preheat oven to 300°F. Put meat into casserole dish with broth, onions, celery and pepper. Mix flour and bread crumbs and stir into liquid. Cover and bake 2 ½ to 3 hours. Serve over rice.

Per serving
490 calories
80 mg cholesterol
607.5 mg sodium
7.0 gm saturated fat
15.1 gm fat

Exchanges per serving
3 bread
3 meat

On the side A mixed green salad, a glass of milk, and fresh fruit for dessert complete this meal nutritiously.

Beef Kabobs

1½ lbs. lean beef, cut into 1-inch cubes
2 tsp. minced garlic
¼ cup minced onion
⅓ cup lemon juice
½ tsp. dry mustard
¾ tsp. chili powder
⅛ tsp. pepper
2 tsp. honey
¾ tsp. ginger
1 tsp. allspice

Place meat in mixing bowl. Combine remaining ingredients and pour over meat; mix thoroughly. Let stand for 1 hour. Thread meat on skewers. Broil, turning occasionally, until desired doneness.

Per serving
254 calories
185 mg cholesterol
102 mg sodium
4.25 gm saturated fat
13.3 gm fat

Exchanges per serving
3 meat

On the side Serve with fresh tomatoes, a slice of bread, a glass of milk, and mixed fruit dessert for a meal that's delicious and nutritious.

1 lb. ground beef
1½ cup sliced onions
1 can chicken noodle soup
1 can mushroom soup
⅛ tsp. pepper
2 cups water
1 cup uncooked rice

Preheat oven to 350°F. Brown meat and onions. Add soups, water, and rice; mix. Place in a casserole dish. Bake for 1 hour 45 minutes.

Per serving
339 calories
50 mg cholesterol
689 mg sodium
4.8 gm saturated fat
13.8 gm fat

Exchanges per serving
2 bread
1½ fat
2 meat
½ vegetable

On the side Serve this yummy goulash with a glass of cold, non-fat milk, and finish off the meal with baked apples as dessert.

Burgerwich

1 lb. lean ground beef
¾ cup green pepper, chopped
¼ cup chopped red pepper
¼ cup chopped onions
1 cup tomato sauce
4 tsp. Dijon-style mustard
3 tsp. Worcestershire sauce
1 Tbsp. ketchup
3 hamburger buns, whole wheat

In a skillet, cook meat and drain fat. Add green peppers, red peppers, and onions and cook over medium heat until vegetables are tender. Stir in tomato sauce, mustard, Worcestershire sauce, and ketchup. Bring to a boil. Reduce heat and simmer 10 to 15 minutes. Split hamburger buns in half and toast under broiler. Divide meat mixture among buns for an open-face sandwich.

Per serving
247 calories
68.3 mg cholesterol
371 mg sodium
3.6 gm saturated fat
9.8 gm fat

Exchanges per serving
1 bread
2 meat
1 vegetable

On the side Add a glass of milk and a fruit of your choice.

113 Delicious Easy Oven Stew

Serves 6

¾ lb. round steak, cubed
1 Tbsp. vegetable oil
4 medium potatoes, unpeeled, cut into 1-inch cubes
5 medium carrots, cut into 1½ -inch chunks
1 celery rib, cut into 1-inch chunks
1 large onion, cut into 1-inch chunks
14½ oz. can chunky stewed tomatoes
3 Tbsp. quick-cooking tapioca
1 tsp. browning sauce
¼ tsp. pepper
1 cup frozen peas

Preheat oven to 300°F. In a Dutch oven, brown the steak in oil. Add the next eight ingredients; cover and bake for 4 to 5 hours, stirring twice. Add the peas during the last 30 minutes of baking.

Per serving
254 calories
34 mg cholesterol
352 mg sodium
1.8 gm saturated fat
6.6 gm fat

Exchanges per serving
2 bread
2 vegetables
2 meat
½ fat

On the side Serve with fresh fruit and a glass of milk to round out this meal.

Dilled Round Steak

1 lb. beef round steak
¾ cup water
⅔ cup sliced onions
2 tsp. lime juice
½ tsp. instant beef bouillon granules
½ tsp. garlic powder
½ tsp. dried dillweed
⅛ tsp. pepper
1 Tbsp. cornstarch mixed with 2 Tbsp. water

Cut meat into 4 servings. In nonstick skillet, brown meat on medium-high heat. Add water, onion, lime juice, bouillon granules, garlic powder, dillweed, and pepper. Bring to a boil, then reduce heat. Cover and simmer for 30 to 40 minutes. Stir cornstarch mixture into juices. Cook until thick and bubbly.

Per serving
185 calories
72 mg cholesterol
271 mg sodium
1.9 gm saturated fat
5.3 gm fat

Exchanges per serving
4 meat

On the side Steamed cauliflower florets, a slice of bread, a glass of milk and chilled peaches for dessert make this meal nutritionally balanced.

2 Tbsp. margarine
3 lbs. lean round beef steak, cubed
½ cup flour
1 cup chopped onions
2 cups fresh, sliced mushrooms
2 tsp. crushed garlic
1 cup light sour cream
⅛ tsp. pepper
6 cups cooked noodles

In large skillet, melt margarine. Lightly coat each piece of meat with flour. Saute meat until all sides are brown; remove and set aside. Add onions, mushrooms, and garlic; saute until tender. Add sour cream and pepper and stir. Put beef back into skillet. Heat thoroughly. Serve over noodles.

Per serving
337 calories
87 mg cholesterol
137 mg sodium
3.1 gm saturated fat
16.9 gm fat

Exchanges per serving
1½ bread
1½ fat
3½ meat
½ vegetable

On the side A glass of milk and a piece of fruit make this meal a standalone, nutritionally.

Fluffy Meat Loaf

1 lb. lean ground beef
1 egg
⅓ cup oatmeal
⅓ cup water
1 small potato, grated
1 tsp. dried parsley flakes
⅛ tsp. pepper
1 Tbsp. minced onion

Preheat oven to 350°F. Combine all ingredients in bowl. Mix well. Shape into loaf on a shallow baking dish. Bake 1 hour.

Per serving
320 calories
156 mg cholesterol
116 mg sodium
7.7 gm saturated fat
13.3 gm fat

Exchanges per serving
1 bread
3 meat

On the side Steamed fresh spinach, a glass of milk, and melon balls for dessert make this meal nutritionally complete.

1 egg white
2½ Tbsp. water
3 Tbsp. herb-seasoned bread crumbs
¾ tsp. dried oregano
⅛ tsp. salt
⅛ tsp. pepper
1 lb. lean ground beef
1 small cucumber, chopped
⅔ cup tomato sauce
1 tsp. minced onion

Preheat broiler. In a mixing bowl, beat egg white and water together until combined. Add bread crumbs. Stir in ½ tsp. oregano, salt, and pepper. Add beef, then mix well. Shape meat mixture into four patties. Place patties on broiling pan and broil until desired doneness. While meat is broiling, combine cucumber, tomato sauce, onion, and ¼ tsp. oregano. Heat mixture until bubbly, stirring all the while. Serve meat patties topped with tomato sauce mixture.

Per serving
290 calories
165 mg cholesterol
156 mg sodium
5.75 gm saturated fat
15.0 gm fat

Exchanges per serving
3 meat
1 vegetable

On the side Fresh tomatoes and lettuce leaves are delicious with these burgers, either on top or on the side. Add a glass of milk and a fruit for dessert to make the meal nutritionally balanced.

German Casserole

Serves 6 **118**

1 14-oz. can sauerkraut and juice
½ cup water
½ cup uncooked rice
¾ cup chopped onion
1 lb. lean ground beef
¼ cup finely diced green pepper
¼ cup low-sodium beef broth
1 8-oz. can low-sodium tomato sauce
¼ tsp. black pepper

Preheat oven to 350°F. In a casserole dish, pour in sauerkraut and its juices and add water. Sprinkle with rice, onion, beef and green pepper. Pour broth over mixture, then pour tomato sauce over the top. Sprinkle with black pepper. Bake uncovered for 1½ hours.

Per serving
200 calories
68 mg cholesterol
597 mg sodium
3.31 gm saturated fat
8.8 gm fat

Exchanges per serving
2½ meat
1 vegetable

On the side A slice of rye bread, a glass of milk, and a fresh pear make this meal nutritionally complete.

1 lb. lean ground beef

2 eggs, beaten

1 cup plain bread crumbs

4 Tbsp. minced onion

4 Tbsp. pickle relish

2 tsp. Worcestershire sauce

1 cup sauerkraut, drained and chopped

½ cup part-skim Swiss cheese, shredded

Preheat oven to 350°F. In a bowl, combine all ingredients, except sauerkraut and cheese; mix thoroughly. Spread mixture to form a 6 x 8-inch rectangle. Spread sauerkraut over meat. Sprinkle half the cheese over the sauerkraut. Start at the short end and roll up meat like a jelly roll. Transfer to a pan and bake for 30 to 40 minutes. Sprinkle remaining cheese on top and bake until cheese is melted.

Per serving
344 calories
169 mg cholesterol
796 mg sodium
7.28 gm saturated fat
16.45 gm fat

Exchanges per serving
1 bread
3 meat
4 vegetable

On the side Boiled spaghetti squash, a glass of nonfat milk, and cantaloupe melon balls, 1 cup per person, complete this meal nutritionally.

Goulash

1 lb. lean ground beef
1 8-oz. can low-sodium tomato sauce
2 Tbsp. ketchup
¼ tsp. pepper
¼ tsp. salt
1 7-oz. package Creamettes macaroni

In skillet, brown beef; pour off fat. Add tomato sauce, ketchup, salt and pepper. Mix. Cook noodles according to package directions; drain. Stir noodles into beef mixture. Heat thoroughly.

Per serving
201 calories
68 mg cholesterol
140 mg sodium
3.5 gm saturated fat
9.0 gm fat

Exchanges per serving
1 bread
2 meat

On the side Cabbage salad with carrots, a glass of nonfat milk, and a fresh pear complete this meal nutritionally.

121 Green Pepper Steak

Serves 4

½ lb. lean round beef steak
⅛ cup soy sauce
1 tsp. minced garlic
⅛ tsp. ground ginger
2 Tbsp. vegetable oil
½ cup chopped green onions
½ cup chopped red pepper
½ cup chopped green pepper
½ cup chopped celery
1 tsp. cornstarch
½ cup water
2 cups cooked rice

Cut beef into thin strips. Combine soy sauce, garlic, and ginger; mix. Add beef and toss. Heat oil in skillet. Add beef mixture and stir-fry over high heat until brown. Cover and simmer until meat is tender. Turn up heat and add vegetables and stir-fry until crisp-tender. Mix cornstarch with water; add to skillet. Stir and cook until thickened. Serve with rice.

Per serving
260 calories
38.5 mg cholesterol
675 mg sodium
2.75 gm saturated fat
12.1 gm fat

Exchanges per serving
1 bread
2 meat
1 vegetable

On the side Combine this zesty steak with a glass of milk and a serving of your favorite fruit and you have a meal that is delicious and nutritionally complete.

1 lb. lean ground beef

1 cup chopped onions

1 28-oz. can tomato purée

1 tsp. garlic

1½ tsp. dried basil

½ tsp. sugar

8 oz. package of macaroni, cooked

¼ cup grated Parmesan cheese

In a large saucepan, cook beef and onions until beef is browned, stirring frequently. Drain. Add tomato puree, garlic, basil, and sugar. Simmer for 20 minutes. Add macaroni to mixture and sprinkle with Parmesan cheese.

Per serving
341 calories
110 mg cholesterol
124 mg sodium
6.1 gm saturated fat
15.7 gm fat

Exchanges per serving
1 bread
3 meat
1 vegetable

On the side You need only drink a glass of nonfat milk and choose your favorite fruit as dessert for this meal to be nutritionally complete.

1 Tbsp. vegetable oil
1½ lb. lean veal shoulder, cut into cubes
1 cup chopped onions
¼ cup water
1 Tbsp. lemon juice
⅛ tsp. pepper
⅛ tsp. crushed fennel seed
¼ cup chopped green onions
1 10 oz. package frozen spinach

In skillet, heat oil; brown veal. Add onion, cook until tender. Pour off fat. Add water, lemon juice, pepper, and crushed fennel seed. Cover and simmer until veal is tender. Add green onions and spinach. More water may be added if needed. Simmer until spinach is tender.

Per serving
230 calories
124 mg cholesterol
145 mg sodium
2.9 gm saturated fat
9.0 gm fat

Exchanges per serving
4 meat
½ fat
1 vegetable

On the side Complete this meal nutritionally by serving each person a slice of bread, a glass of milk, and a fresh pear.

Moist Meat Loaf

1 lb. lean ground beef
⅔ cup oatmeal
½ cup skim milk
1 egg
⅓ cup chopped onions
1 Tbsp. mustard
1 Tbsp. Worcestershire sauce
½ tsp. black pepper
¼ cup ketchup

Preheat oven to 350°F. In a large bowl, mix all the ingredients together; blend well. Shape into a loaf and place in a loaf pan. Bake for 1½ hours.

Per serving
229 calories
109 mg cholesterol
391 mg sodium
5.3 gm saturated fat
11.3 gm fat

Exchanges per serving
1 bread
2 meat

On the side Onions, mushrooms, and green peppers, sautéed in a little margarine, a glass of milk, and baked apple dessert complete this meal nutritionally.

Nonstick cooking spray
1 lb. veal steak, ¾ inch thick
1 Tbsp. flour
⅔ cup water
1 cup sliced, fresh mushrooms
¼ cup chopped onions
1 Tbsp. lemon juice

Spray skillet with cooking spray. Add steak and brown on both sides. Cover and simmer 30 to 35 minutes or until tender. Remove veal and keep warm. Stir flour into meat juices. Increase heat and gradually add water until smooth and thickened. Add mushrooms, onions, and lemon juice. Cook 5 minutes, stirring frequently. Spoon over veal.

Per serving
209 calories
119 mg cholesterol
98 mg sodium
2.7 gm saturated fat
7.2 gm fat

Exchanges per serving
4 meat

On the side Green beans, simply steamed, a slice of your favorite bread, a glass of nonfat milk, and fresh fruit as dessert complete this meal nutritionally.

Oven Porcupines

1 lb. lean ground beef
½ cup uncooked rice
1½ cup water
½ cup chopped onion
½ tsp. celery salt
⅛ tsp. garlic powder
⅛ tsp. pepper
1 15 oz. can low-sodium tomato sauce
1 Tbsp. Worcestershire sauce

Preheat oven to 350°F. In bowl, mix beef, rice, ½ cup water, onion, celery salt, garlic powder, and pepper. Shape mixture into 10 balls. Cook in skillet until brown on all sides. Drain. Place meatballs in 8 x 8-inch dish. Mix remaining ingredients; pour over meat-balls. Cover and bake for 50 to 55 minutes.

Per serving
277 calories
103 mg cholesterol
414 mg sodium
5.3 gm saturated fat
13.3 gm fat

Exchanges per serving
1 bread
1 fat
2 meat

On the side Choose green beans, carrots, or mixed vegetables, a glass of milk, and fruit to make this meal a nutritionally balanced one.

127 Quick Steak Stew

Serves 4

¾ lb. boneless beef round steak
¼ tsp. pepper
1½ cup low-sodium beef broth
1 tsp. beef bouillon
1 9-oz. package frozen green beans
2 cups frozen hash brown potatoes
   with onions and peppers
1 cup tomato sauce
¾ tsp. sugar
1 Tbsp. cornstarch

Trim fat from beef and cut into bite size pieces.
Sprinkle with pepper. In a skillet, brown meat over
medium heat. Add beef broth. Bring to a boil and
reduce heat. Add beef bouillon; cover and simmer for
15 minutes. Rinse and drain beans and potatoes. Add
beans and potatoes to skillet; simmer for 10 minutes.
Stir together tomato sauce, sugar, and cornstarch and
add to meat mixture. Cook and stir until bubbly and
thickened.

Per serving
302 calories
93 mg cholesterol
583 mg sodium
4.5 gm saturated fat
10.0 gm fat

Exchanges per serving
1 bread
2½ meat
1 vegetable

On the side Serve this with a glass of milk and a single-cup
serving of mixed melon balls for dessert for a healthful and
nutritionally balanced meal.

Rolled Veal Loaf

2 lbs. ground veal
¾ cup plain bread crumbs
¾ cup chopped onions
1 egg, beaten
1 Tbsp. minced garlic
1 tsp. dried parsley flakes
1 Tbsp. low-cal Thousand Island dressing
1 tsp. oregano
1½ tsp. chili powder
⅛ tsp. salt
⅛ tsp. pepper
1 cup fresh, chopped mushrooms
½ cup part-skim mozzarella cheese

Preheat oven to 350°F. In a mixing bowl, combine all
ingredients, except cheese and mushrooms; mix well.
Shape meat mixture into a 20 x 9-inch rectangle.
Sprinkle with cheese and mushrooms. Roll meat jelly-
roll style, starting from 9-inch end. Transfer to a loaf
pan. Bake for 1 hour.

Per serving
365 calories
41 mg cholesterol
237 mg sodium
8.82 gm saturated fat
18.5 gm fat

Exchanges per serving:
½ bread
½ fat
4 meat

On the side Serve this with corn on the cob, and mix up your
favorite fresh fruits for dessert for a nutritionally balanced
meal.

Nonstick cooking spray
2 cups yellow onion, chopped
5 cloves garlic, minced
3½ lb. eye of round, fat trimmed
1½ cup V-8 juice
3 tsp. beef bouillon granules
1 cup dry red wine
1 tsp. dried parsley
4 whole cloves
3 bay leaves
1 tsp. salt
1 tsp. paprika
½ tsp. black pepper
1 lb. baby carrots
1 Tbsp. cornstarch
¾ cup water
12 cups egg noodles, cooked

Spray a Dutch oven with cooking spray. Over medium heat, add onions and garlic. Cook until onions are tender. Place in a bowl and set aside. Recoat Dutch oven with cooking spray. Add beef and brown. Add reserved onion mixture, V-8 juice, beef granules, wine, parsley, cloves, bay leaves, salt, paprika, and pepper. Cover and simmer for 2½ hours. Do not boil. Stir in carrots, adding ½ cup water if needed. Cover and continue to cook for an additional 1-1½ hours or until beef is tender. Remove beef and slice thin. Combine cornstarch with remaining water. Mix well. Add to sauce and bring to a boil. Cook 1 minute. Serve beef with noodles and sauce.

Per serving

426 calories
128 mg cholesterol
596 mg sodium
3.8 gm saturated fat
12 gm fat

Exchanges per serving

2½ bread
4 meat
½ fat
1 vegetable

On the side A glass of milk and mixed melon balls, 1 cup per serving, complete this meal.

2 cups boiling water
⅓ cup cracked wheat
¾ cup ground lean beef
¾ cup chopped cucumber
⅓ cup finely chopped, fresh parsley
½ cup sliced green onion
2 tomatoes finely chopped
⅛ tsp. salt
⅛ tsp. black pepper
3 Tbsp. lemon juice

In medium bowl, pour boiling water over cracked wheat. Let stand until water is absorbed—about one hour. Drain. Cook beef and drain fat. Combine all ingredients together and mix with a spoon.

Per serving
194 calories
24 mg cholesterol
20.5 mg sodium
1.25 gm saturated fat
3.36 gm fat

Exchanges per serving
1 bread
1 meat
1 vegetable

On the side Fresh peaches with yogurt for dessert make this meal nutritionally complete.

Teriyaki Beef with Broccoli

Serves 4 **131**

1 16-oz. package frozen broccoli, baby carrots, and
   water chestnuts
1 lb. beef cubed steak
½ cup water
3 Tbsp. teriyaki sauce
2 tsp. soy sauce
½ tsp. five spice powder
½ tsp. minced garlic
2 cups cooked rice

Rinse and drain vegetables. Cut beef into bite-size
strips, In a bowl, combine water, teriyaki sauce, soy
sauce, five spice powder, and garlic. In a skillet, stir-
fry beef on high until browned. Add vegetables and
stir-fry for 3 to 4 minutes. Reduce heat. Stir in sauce
and cook until thick and bubbly. Serve over rice.

Per serving
331 calories
123 mg cholesterol
1229 mg sodium
2.8 gm saturated fat
7.0 gm fat

Exchanges per serving
1 bread
3 meat
1 vegetable

On the side A glass of nonfat milk and some fresh fruit for
dessert round out this meal nutritionally.

Beef & Veal ■ 141

1 lb. lean ground beef
1 Tbsp. minced onion
2 tsp. parsley flakes
1 6 oz. can low-sodium tomato paste
3 cups water
1 tsp. chili powder
½ cup sliced, fresh mushrooms
7 oz. package macaroni

Brown beef in skillet; drain fat. Add onions, parsley flakes, tomato paste, water, chili powder, mushrooms and macaroni. Bring to a boil. Cover and simmer until macaroni is tender.

Per serving
273 calories
63.4 mg cholesterol
68.4 mg sodium
1.7 gm saturated fat
5.4 gm fat

Exchanges per serving
1 bread
2 meat
1 vegetable

On the side Mixed fruit with a dollop of nonfat yogurt offers a refreshing dessert for this meal and completes it nutritionally.

Veal Barley Stew

Nonstick cooking spray
1 lb. lean boneless veal, cubed
3 cups sliced fresh mushrooms
1 cup chopped onions
1 tsp. minced garlic
2 12-oz. cans vegetable juice
1 cup sliced carrots
1 cup sliced celery
2 cups potatoes, cubed
½ cup pearl barley
1 bay leaf
¾ tsp. dried basil

Spray a skillet with nonstick spray. Brown veal and remove from skillet. Cook mushrooms, onion, and garlic until mushrooms are tender. Drain off any fat. Stir in meat, vegetable juice, carrots, celery, potatoes, barley, bay leaf, and basil. Bring to a boil. Reduce heat and simmer for 45 minutes. Discard bay leaf.

Per serving
359 calories
77 mg cholesterol
331 mg sodium
5.0 gm saturated fat
19.0 gm fat

Exchanges per serving
1 bread
3 meat
1 vegetable

On the side A glass of milk and a serving of fresh fruit complete this meal nutritionally.

134 Veal Chops

Serves 4

Nonstick cooking spray
4 veal rib chops
1 Tbsp. margarine
½ cup chopped onion
1 tsp. minced garlic
4 cups sliced, fresh mushrooms
1 16-oz. can low-sodium stewed tomatoes
⅛ tsp. ground pepper
¼ tsp. sage
1 Tbsp. dry red wine

Spray skillet with nonstick cooking spray. Brown chops on both sides. Remove from skillet. Add margarine, onion, and garlic to skillet and cook until soft. Add mushrooms and cook until soft. Add tomatoes and their juice, pepper, sage, and wine; bring to a boil. Reduce heat. Return chops to skillet and simmer, turning occasionally, until veal is tender. Spoon sauce over veal.

Per serving
310 calories
87 mg cholesterol
122 mg sodium
6.5 gm saturated fat
14.0 gm fats

Exchanges per serving
1 fat
3 meat
1 vegetable

On the side A side dish of boiled spaghetti squash is delicious with this veal dish. A glass of milk and your pick of fresh fruits complete the meal nutritionally.

Veal with Peppers

2 Tbsp. vegetable oil
4 veal cutlets
1 large red pepper cut into strips
1 large green pepper cut into strips
¾ cup chopped onions
1 tsp. minced garlic
¼ tsp. ground pepper
½ tsp. sage
¼ cup water

In skillet, heat oil. Brown veal; remove from skillet.
Reduce heat and add red peppers, green peppers,
onion, garlic, sage, ground pepper. Cook until peppers
are soft. Return veal to skillet. Add water and cook
until veal is tender.

Per serving
265 calories
87 mg cholesterol
76 mg sodium
4.7 gm saturated fat
16.0 gm fat

Exchanges per serving
1 fat
3 meat
1 vegetable

On the side Add a serving of white rice and offer fresh fruit for
dessert to make this meal nutritionally complete.

1 breast of veal, about 4 lbs. (3 lbs. cooked weight)
2 cups cooked rice
1 tsp. dried parsley flakes
½ tsp. grated lime rind
1 tsp. basil
⅛ tsp. salt
⅛ tsp. pepper
⅛ tsp. paprika
½ tsp. garlic powder

Preheat oven to 350°F. Split breast of veal to form
pocket for stuffing. Trim off all fat. Combine rice,
parsley, lime rind, basil, salt, and pepper. Stuff into
veal pocket. Place veal in a roasting pan. Sprinkle
with paprika and garlic powder. Roast for 2½ hours or
until browned and tender.

Per serving
265 calories
133 mg cholesterol
545 mg sodium
2.1 gm saturated fat
7.6 gm fat

Exchanges per serving
½ bread
5 meat

On the side Asparagus, steamed gently over boiling water, and a
dessert of fresh pears complete this meal nutritionally.

Veal with Zucchini

6 veal cutlets
¾ cup skim milk
⅓ cup whole-wheat bread crumbs
1 cup chopped tomatoes
¼ tsp. oregano
¼ tsp. sage
2 medium zucchinis, sliced

Dip cutlets in milk, then in bread crumbs. Brown in nonstick pan. Add tomatoes, oregano, and sage. Cover and simmer for 30 minutes. Add zucchini and simmer for another 15 minutes.

Per serving
276 calories
88 mg cholesterol
208 mg sodium
4.16 gm saturated fat
10.0 gm fat

Exchanges per serving
3 meat
1 vegetable

On the side A side dish of brown rice, or a slice of your favorite bread, a glass of nonfat milk, and fresh fruit make this meal a complete and nutritionally balanced one.

1 Tbsp. vegetable oil
3 cups broccoli florets
1 cup sliced carrots
½ cup sliced onions
1 cup green pepper, chopped
1 cup sliced zucchini
12 oz. broiled sirloin steak, cut into strips
2 Tbsp. soy sauce
1 tsp. cornstarch
½ tsp. sugar

In large skillet, heat oil; add broccoli, carrots, onions, green pepper, and zucchini. Stir frequently and quickly until vegetables are tender-crisp. Stir in beef strips. In small bowl, combine soy sauce, sugar, and cornstarch; add to beef mixture and cook until sauce is thickened, stirring frequently.

Per serving
274 calories
76 mg cholesterol
617 mg sodium
3.5 gm saturated fat
11.6 gm fat

Exchanges per serving
1 fat
3½ meat
2 vegetable

On the side A serving of white rice (½ cup per person), a glass of milk, and fresh fruit for dessert, and you have a nutritionally complete meal.

Seafood
& Fish

1 (4 lb.) whole bass
3½ quarts water
1 cup sliced carrots
1 cup sliced celery
1 tsp. salt
6 peppercorns
1 bay leaf
⅛ tsp. thyme
1 tsp. lemon pepper

Thoroughly clean and scale fish. Wrap fish loosely in foil; do not seal. In 5-quart saucepan, place foil-wrapped fish in the water and add remaining ingredients. Bring to a boil and reduce heat. Cook fish 15 minutes. Let stand in cooking liquid until ready to serve.

Per serving
226 calories
128 mg cholesterol
533 mg sodium
1.5 gm saturated fat
6.87 gm fat

Exchanges per serving
3 meat
1 vegetable

On the side Serve this tasty fish with a side dish of brown rice, and create a fresh fruit dessert using yogurt and peaches, and you'll have a meal that's delicious and nutritious.

Baked Cod

2 lbs. cod
½ cup sliced green onions
¾ cup sliced celery
1 tsp. minced garlic
1 tomato, sliced
⅛ tsp. lemon pepper
¾ tsp. dried thyme
½ tsp. dried basil
½ cup low-sodium tomato sauce

Preheat oven to 350°F. In baking dish, place a layer of onions, celery, garlic, and tomato slices. Place cod on top of layer, and cover fish with a repeat layer. Sprinkle with lemon pepper, thyme, and basil. Pour tomato sauce over top of fish. Cover and bake for 25 minutes or until fish is done.

Per serving
211 calories
82 mg cholesterol
176 mg sodium
0.26 gm saturated fat
1.3 gm fat

Exchanges per serving
4 meat

On the side A side dish of broccoli and cauliflower, steamed just until tender, and a dessert of fresh fruit with yogurt complete this meal nutritionally.

4 oz. frozen crab meat, thawed, drained
⅔ cup part-skim cheddar cheese, shredded
⅓ cup chopped green onions
4 eggs
¾ cup evaporated skim milk
½ tsp. dry mustard
⅛ tsp. black pepper
½ tsp. lemon juice
⅛ tsp. paprika

Preheat oven to 400°F. In medium bowl, combine crab meat, cheese and green onions. Pour crab meat in an 8-inch glass pie plate; press mixture over bottom and up sides. In mixing bowl, beat, using a wire whisk, eggs, milk, mustard, pepper, and lemon juice together. Pour over crab meat mixture. Sprinkle with paprika and bake for 30 to 35 minutes.

Per serving
158 calories
266 mg cholesterol
376 mg sodium
2.42 gm saturated fat
7.48 gm fat

Exchanges per serving
2 meat

On the side Serve this elegant quiche on a plate surrounded by alternating points of honeydew melon slices and fresh strawberries. A freshly baked muffin, bread, or a roll, and a glass of milk make this meal nutritionally complete.

Baked Ratatouille and Fish

1 medium size zucchini, sliced
1 small eggplant, cut into chunks
1 cup yellow pepper, chopped
1 cup red pepper, chopped
3 tsp. dry basil leaves
1 tsp. oregano
1 Tbsp. vegetable oil
1 lb. white-flesh fish fillets
⅓ cup part-skim Havarti cheese, shredded

Preheat oven to 425°F. In shallow 3-quart baking dish, combine zucchini, eggplant, yellow and red peppers, basil, oregano, and oil. Cover and bake for 40 minutes. Push vegetables to sides of the dish and lay fish in the center. Cover and bake for 20 to 25 minutes. Sprinkle with cheese and bake until cheese melts.

Per serving
226 calories
22 mg cholesterol
177 mg sodium
4.6 gm saturated fat
11.1 gm fat

Exchanges per serving
3 meat
1 vegetable

On the side Serve this with a ½ cup of white rice per person, and finish the meal with slices of juicy, ripe oranges. A glass of milk with this meal makes it nutritionally complete.

1 pkg. (11½ oz.) frozen fish, thawed
2 Tbsp. lemon juice
⅛ tsp. salt
⅛ tsp. lemon pepper
⅛ tsp. paprika
2 Tbsp. light mayonnaise
2 Tbsp. plain low-fat yogurt
1 tsp. dried dillweed
1 tomato, sliced
½ tsp. dried parsley flakes, crushed

Preheat oven to 450°F. Place fish in a shallow baking dish. Brush fish with lemon juice; sprinkle with salt, lemon pepper, and paprika. Bake for 10 minutes or until fish flakes easily. Meanwhile, in a mixing bowl, stir together mayonnaise, yogurt, dillweed, and parsley. Spoon over fish. Serve with tomatoes.

Per serving
168 calories
1.2 mg cholesterol
271 mg sodium
0.25 gm saturated fat
11.2 gm fat

Exchanges per serving
1 fat
2 lean meat

On the side Serve this tangy fish dish with green noodles. Add a tossed salad, some fruit and yogurt for dessert, and the meal is nutritionally complete.

Fish and Vegetables

Serves 4 **144**

1 tsp. grated orange peel
1 cup orange juice
¼ cup soy sauce
1 tsp. ground ginger
3 medium carrots, cut in julienne strips
1 pkg. (11½ oz.) frozen fish portions, thawed
1 cup sliced zucchini
2 tsp. cornstarch
4 Tbsp. water

In a skillet, combine orange peel, orange juice, soy sauce, and ginger. Add carrot strips and bring to a boil. Reduce heat and simmer for 5 minutes. Push carrots to the side of the skillet and add fish. Arrange sliced zucchini around fish. Bring to a boil. Reduce heat, cover and simmer until fish flakes easily. Remove vegetables and fish from skillet. Stir together cornstarch and water. Add to orange juice mixture; cook and stir until thickened and bubbly. Return fish and vegetables to skillet. Heat through. Spoon glaze atop. Serve.

Per serving
216 calories
0 mg cholesterol
1036 mg sodium
0 gm saturated fat
10 gm fat

Exchanges per serving
3 meat
1 vegetable

On the side The oriental-style flavor of this dish recommends white rice as an accompaniment. Fresh fruit with yogurt completes the meal.

1 lb. fresh fish
½ cup herb-seasoned bread crumbs
⅓ cup grated Parmesan cheese
1 Tbsp. margarine, melted
⅛ tsp. pepper

Preheat oven to 450°F. Cut fish into four portions. Combine bread crumbs, Parmesan cheese, margarine, and pepper. Place fish in a nonstick shallow baking pan. Sprinkle with bread crumb mixture. Bake for 25 to 30 minutes.

Per serving
230 calories
10 mg cholesterol
262 mg sodium
2.25 gm saturated fat
6.7 gm fat

Exchanges per serving
½ bread
½ fat
3 meat

On the side Boiled squash makes a nice addition to these cheesy fillets. Serve some fruit as dessert with a glass of nonfat milk and the meal is nutritionally balanced.

Wine Baked Fillets

1 lb. frozen or fresh fish fillets
dash of salt (to taste)
dash of pepper (to taste)
⅛ tsp. paprika
⅓ cup dry white wine
⅛ tsp. dried oregano, crushed
⅔ cup part-skim shredded Swiss cheese

Preheat oven to 350°F. Place fish in nonstick baking
dish. Season with salt, pepper, and paprika. Pour
wine over fish. Sprinkle with oregano. Bake for
35 minutes. Sprinkle fish with cheese and bake for
10 minutes more.

Per serving
160 calories
39 mg cholesterol
565 mg sodium
2.1 gm saturated fat
9.2 gm fat

Exchanges per serving
3 meat

On the side Boiled spaghetti squash or a mixed broccoli and cauliflower side dish make nice accompaniments to Wine Baked
Fillets. A glass of milk and a fresh fruit of your choice as
dessert complete the meal nutritionally.

Nonstick cooking spray
1 lb. haddock
¼ tsp. salt
¼ cup margarine, melted
⅛ tsp. black pepper
⅛ tsp. paprika
2 Tbsp. lemon juice

Heat oven to 350°F. Spray roasting pan with non-stick spray. Place fish in pan. Sprinkle with salt and melted margarine. Season with pepper and paprika. Bake 20 minutes or until fish flakes easily. Pour lemon juice over fish.

Per serving
200 calories
65.29 mg cholesterol
215 mg sodium
2.1 gm saturated fat
12.07 gm fat

Exchanges per serving
1 fat
3 meat

On the side Eggplant squares, a cabbage salad, fruit, and milk make this meal nutritionally complete.

Crispy Fillets

1 lb. walleye fillets
¾ cup skim milk
⅔ cup herb-seasoned bread crumbs
¼ tsp salt
⅛ tsp. pepper

Preheat the oven to 500°F. Dip fillets in skim
milk and coat with bread crumbs. Season
with salt and pepper. Arrange fillets in baking dish.
Bake 10 to 15 minutes.

Per serving
149 calories
73.75 mg cholesterol
333 mg sodium
0.4 gm saturated fat
1.0 gm fat

Exchanges per serving
½ bread
3 meat

On the side New potatoes in rosemary, steamed broccoli spears,
and mixed melon balls with a garnish of fresh mint
complement the meal. Add a glass of milk for complete nutritional balance.

1 lb. haddock fillets
½ chili pepper, chopped
⅔ cup chopped onion
⅓ cup chopped green pepper
⅓ cup chopped red pepper
1 lb. can low-sodium tomato puree
1½ tsp. basil
½ cup chopped carrots
4 tsp. lemon juice

Preheat oven to 350°F. Mix all the ingredients together, except fish, in a bowl. Pour half the mixture into a baking dish and place fish on top. Pour the remainder of the sauce over the fish. Bake for 25 to 30 minutes.

Per serving
117 calories
43.28 mg cholesterol
79.5 mg sodium
0.08 gm saturated fat
0.63 gm fat

Exchanges per serving
2 meat
1 vegetable

On the side Rice makes a nice side dish with this flavorful fish dish. Some fruit with yogurt as dessert rounds out the meal nutritionally.

1 Tbsp. margarine, divided
2 Tbsp. slivered almonds
4 tsp. flour
⅛ tsp. pepper
8 oz. haddock
1 tsp. lime juice

In a skillet, melt ½ tablespoon margarine. Add almonds and saute until golden; remove and set aside. In a bowl, combine flour and pepper. Sprinkle both sides of fillets with flour and pepper. In same skillet heat ½ tablespoon margarine; add fillets and cook on both sides until brown. Remove, reduce heat to low. Add lime juice and sauteed almonds to skillet and cook until heated. Top fillets with almond mixture.

Per serving
190 calories
65 mg cholesterol
144 mg sodium
1.3 gm saturated fat
10.3 gm fat

Exchanges per serving
2 fat
3 meat

On the side A serving of white rice, some steamed green beans, and a fruit for dessert round out this meal nutritionally.

1 Tbsp. vegetable oil

1 cup chopped onions

¼ cup green onions, sliced

2 lbs. haddock fillets

1 cup diced tomatoes

1 tsp. dried parsley flakes, crushed

⅛ tsp. pepper

½ tsp. garlic powder

3 Tbsp. dry white wine

1 tsp. Italian herb blend

Preheat oven to 375°F. In a skillet, heat oil. Add onions and green onions. Sauté for 3 to 4 minutes. Place onions in an 8-inch square baking dish. Cut fish fillets into 6 portions and place atop of onions. Season fish with pepper and garlic powder. Place tomatoes on top of fish; sprinkle with Italian herbs, parsley flakes and wine. Cover and bake for 20 minutes.

Per serving
216 calories
47.7 mg cholesterol
86 mg sodium
0.86 gm saturated fat
5.86 gm fat

Exchanges per serving
½ fat
4 meat
1 vegetable

On the side Rice is really nice with this spicy Italian seafood dish. Milk and fruit are all you need to make the meal nutritionally complete.

Haddock with Crumbs

2 lb. haddock fillets
⅛ tsp. salt
⅛ tsp. pepper
½ cup margarine
2 cups herb-seasoned bread crumbs
¼ tsp. oregano
¼ tsp. marjoram
1 tsp. grated lemon rind

Preheat oven to 350°F. Cut fish into 6 servings.
Arrange fish on a nonstick baking pan. Sprinkle with
salt and pepper and pour ¼ of margarine over fish.
Mix bread crumbs, oregano, marjoram, and lemon
rind together and sprinkle over top of fish. Bake for 20
to 25 minutes.

Per serving
396 calories
87.1 mg cholesterol
594 mg sodium
3.1 gm saturated fat
17.8 gm fat

Exchanges per serving
1½ bread
3½ fat
4 meat

On the side Steamed carrot rounds make a colorful and healthful
side dish to this seafood main course. A dessert of fruit and
yogurt complete the meal nutritionally.

This is a LOW FAT DISH

¼ cup finely chopped onions
½ tsp. minced garlic
    1 cup chopped carrots
    ⅔ cup sliced fresh mushrooms
    ½ cup chopped tomatoes
    1 tsp. dried parsley flakes
    1 tsp. basil
⅛ tsp. pepper
1 lb. haddock
3 Tbsp. lime juice

In skillet, simmer all ingredients, except fish and lime juice. Cook until carrots are tender. Add fish and lime juice, spooning vegetables over fish. Cover and cook until fish is flaky; about 15 minutes.

Per serving
163 calories
24 mg cholesterol
135 mg sodium
0.18 gm saturated fat
2.1 gm fat

Exchanges per serving
2 meat
1 vegetable

On the side Serve this fish, which is a little heavier than a sole fillet, with a ½ cup of white rice, and choose a refreshing light-tasting fruit or combination of fruits for dessert. A glass of milk or some yogurt as a fruit topping make this meal nutritionally complete.

Baked Halibut with Sauce

Serves 4 **154**

4 halibut steaks
1 Tbsp. vegetable oil
1 cup chopped onions
1 cup chopped green onions
1 tsp. dried parsley flakes
1 tsp. garlic, minced
1 8 oz. can low-sodium tomato sauce
⅛ tsp. pepper

Preheat oven to 375°F. Place halibut in 9 x 13-inch baking dish. In skillet, heat oil and sauté onions until tender. Add remaining ingredients and simmer for 10 minutes. Pour onion mixture over halibut. Bake 20 to 25 minutes.

Per serving
155 calories
27 mg cholesterol
58 mg sodium
0.5 gm saturated fat
3.5 gm fat

Exchanges per serving
3 meat

On the side A serving of long-grain wild rice is a delicious addition to this seafood main dish. A side salad and some fruit for dessert make the meal complete nutritionally.

Seafood & Fish ■ 165

1 lb. halibut
½ cup lemon juice
¾ cup water
¼ cup skim milk
1 Tbsp. flour
½ tsp. dried tarragon
1 tsp. minced onion
⅛ tsp. basil
⅛ black pepper
½ tsp. sage
⅛ tsp. Tabasco sauce

Marinate fish in lemon juice for about 1 hour. Broil fish until done; keep fish warm. In saucepan, add water, milk, and flour; stir until smooth. Cook over low heat until slightly thickened. Add seasonings; cook 5 minutes longer. Pour sauce over fish portions.

Per serving
150 calories
37.6 mg cholesterol
70 mg sodium
0.4 gm saturated fat
2.7 gm fat

Exchanges per serving
3 meat

On the side A serving of colorful and healthful sliced beets provide a ½ bread exchange and only 75 calories as an accompaniment to this broiled fish dish. A glass of nonfat milk and a fresh fruit complement the tastes and complete the meal nutritionally.

Citrus Halibut

1 lb. halibut steaks
1 Tbsp. margarine
½ cup sliced green onions
1 tsp. minced garlic
1 tsp. grated orange peel
⅛ tsp. pepper
⅓ cup orange juice
4 tsp. lemon juice

Preheat oven to 400°F. Arrange fish in baking dish. In skillet, heat margarine and cook onion and garlic. Stir in orange peel and pepper. Spread over fish. Sprinkle orange juice and lemon juice over fish. Bake, covered, for 20 minutes or until fish flakes easily. Pour juice over fish.

Per serving
168 calories
36 mg cholesterol
98 mg sodium
0.89 gm saturated fat
5.6 gm fat

Exchanges per serving
3 meat

On the side Baked squash on the side, a mixed vegetable of your choice, or a side salad, some fruit and a glass of milk make this meal nutritionally complete.

2 lb. halibut, skinned
1 cup radishes
10 scallions, chopped
1 Tbsp. fresh ginger, chopped
3 tsp. soy sauce
2 Tbsp. rice wine
1 tsp. light extra virgin olive oil

Preheat oven to 400°F. Remove bone from halibut. Cut into 4 equal portions, cover and refrigerate. Trim the stem and wash the radishes. Cut into quarters. Place the fish in a glass baking dish large enough to hold the fish in one layer. Scatter the radishes and scallions around the fish and sprinkle the fish with the ginger. In a small dish combine the soy sauce, rice wine, and oil; spoon over the fish. Cover with a lid or aluminum foil, and bake for 20 minutes. Remove fish, radishes, and scallions and serve. Spoon juices over fish.

Per serving
291 calories
73 mg cholesterol
344 mg sodium
0.9 gm saturated fat
6.6 gm fat

Exchanges per serving
5 meat
½ vegetable

On the side New potatoes in rosemary, steamed broccoli spears, and mixed melon balls complete the meal.

Halibut Steaks à la Citrus

1 lb. halibut steaks
2 tsp. finely shredded orange peel
⅔ cup orange juice
1 tsp. cooking oil
½ tsp. dried dillweed
⅛ tsp. pepper

Cut fish into four portions and place in a shallow baking dish. Combine orange peel, orange juice, oil, dillweed, and pepper; pour over fish. Cover and marinate in refrigerator for 1 hour. Place fish on broiling pan and brush with marinade. Broil until fish is flaky. Brush often with marinade.

Per serving
123 calories
27 mg cholesterol
46 mg sodium
1.0 gm saturated fat
3.0 gm fat

Exchanges per serving
2 meat

On the side Zucchini cooked al dente is a delicious side offering to this zesty fish entrée. A dinner roll or slice of your favorite bread, some fruit and yogurt as dessert, and you have a meal that's nutritionally complete.

159 Fish Fillets in Sherry Mushroom Sauce *Serves 5*

2 Tbsp. margarine
1 cup sliced fresh mushrooms
⅓ cup chopped green onions
1½ lbs. halibut
1 tsp. cornstarch
⅓ cup water
2 Tbsp. skim milk
¼ cup sherry
1 Tbsp. soy sauce
1 tsp. garlic
½ tsp. ground ginger

In skillet, heat margarine and sauté mushrooms and green onions. Remove and set aside. Add fish to skillet; cover and cook until fish is white in the center. Remove fish and set aside. Stir cornstarch, water, milk, sherry, soy sauce, garlic and ginger; pour into pan and add mushrooms and onions. Bring mixture to a boil. Pour sauce over fish.

Per serving
208 calories
43 mg cholesterol
281 mg sodium
0.85 gm saturated fat
8.0 gm fat

Exchanges per serving
1 fat
3 meat

On the side Long-grain wild rice tastes great with this sherry-flavored seafood entrée. A tossed salad on the side and a fruit compote topped with a dollop of yogurt complete the meal nutritionally.

Five-Spice Fish

2 lbs. halibut fillets
⅔ cup green onions, chopped
1½ Tbsp. fresh ginger, crushed
½ cup soy sauce
1½ Tbsp. sugar
1 Tbsp. sesame oil
½ tsp. ground cinnamon
½ tsp. allspice
¼ tsp. ground cloves
⅛ tsp. anise seed

Cut fish in 2 x 2-inch long slices. Mix fish with onions, ginger, soy sauce, sugar, oil, and spices. Cover and chill for several hours. Broil on both sides until fish is opaque.

Per serving
158 calories
0 mg cholesterol
886.6 mg sodium
0.24 gm saturated fat
4.42 gm fat

Exchanges per serving
3 meat

On the side Stir-fried cabbage adds a complimentary flavor to this eastern-style fish dish. Add a slice of your favorite bread or a ½ cup serving of white rice, a glass of milk, and a serving of fruit for a nutritionally complete meal.

161 Baked Fillet of Sole

Nonstick cooking spray
¾ cup shallots, finely chopped
1 tsp. dried marjoram
6 Tbsp. dry seasoned bread crumbs
¼ tsp. salt
¼ tsp. black pepper
6 5-oz. fillets of sole
¾ cup dry white wine
1 Tbsp. light extra virgin olive oil

Preheat oven to 475°F. Lightly coat a 10 x 13 x 2 inch baking dish with cooking spray. Sprinkle shallots in bottom of baking dish. Set aside. In a small bowl, combine marjoram, bread crumbs, salt, and pepper. Rinse fillets and blot dry. Place in pan and pour the wine over the fillets. Spoon bread crumb mixture evenly over the fillets and drizzle the oil over the top. Bake until fish turns opaque, then turn over to broil setting and broil fish until lightly brown. Spoon pan juices over the fish. Serve immediately.

Per serving
194 calories
67 mg cholesterol
242 mg sodium
0.7 gm saturated fat
3.2 gm fat

Exchanges per serving
3 meat
½ fat

On the side White rice or a baked potato and green beans are perfect accompaniments to this dish. A mixed fruit salad with yogurt for dessert makes the meal complete.

Baked Fish with Cheese Sauce

1 lb. fresh skinless Orange Roughy
1½ Tbsp. margarine
3 Tbsp. herb-seasoned bread crumbs
⅔ cup skim milk
1 Tbsp. flour
⅔ cup part-skim cheddar cheese, shredded
2 tsp. Dijon-style mustard
1 tsp. dried dillweed

Preheat oven to 400°F. Place fish in a nonstick shallow
baking dish. Melt margarine and brush on top of fish.
Top with bread crumbs and bake for 15 minutes or
until fish is flaky. In a saucepan, stir together milk and
flour. Cook until thickened. Add cheese and mustard.
Stir until cheese melts. Divide sauce among four serving plates. Place one portion of fish on each plate, atop
of sauce. Sprinkle with dillweed.

Per serving
295 calories
169 mg cholesterol
313 mg sodium
4.87 gm saturated fat
19 gm fat

Exchanges per serving
½ bread
2 fat
3 meat

On the side Steamed brussel sprouts provide a vegetable
exchange and a nice contrasting flavor to this cheesy fish
entree. Choose some fruit and maybe a glass of nonfat milk to
round out the meal nutritionally and you're all set.

1 lb. orange roughy fillets
⅛ tsp. pepper
⅛ tsp. salt
⅔ cup lemon yogurt, low-fat
⅓ cup green onions, sliced

Preheat oven to 350°F. Arrange fillets in a 9 x 13-inch pan and sprinkle with salt and pepper. Evenly spread yogurt over fish. Sprinkle with green onions. Bake, uncovered, for 18 to 20 minutes, or until fish is opaque in center.

Per serving
170 calories
25 mg cholesterol
171 mg sodium
0.5 gm saturated fat
8.5 gm fat

Exchanges per serving
3 meat

On the side A side of brussel sprouts, steamed until tender, or a tossed salad, a slice of bread, a glass of milk, and some fruit make this meal nutritionally complete.

Roughy with Lime Juice

Serves 4 **164**

1 Tbsp. vegetable oil
1 garlic clove, pressed
2 tsp. dried dillweed
4 Tbsp. lime juice
⅛ cup chopped peanuts
1 lb. Orange Roughy
⅛ tsp. pepper

In a skillet, heat oil and add dill, garlic, lime juice, and peanuts. Sauté for 1 to 2 minutes. Sprinkle fish with pepper and add fish to skillet. Cover and cook fish until done.

Per serving
212 calories
45 mg cholesterol
24 mg sodium
1.4 gm saturated fat
11.2 gm fat

Exchanges per serving
1 fat
3 meat

On the side Eggplant offers a tempting side dish to this nutty-flavored fish dish. A side salad of your favorite raw vegetables, and strawberries and milk, mixed in the blender, make this meal balanced nutritionally.

Seafood & Fish ■ 175

1½ lb. flounder
1½ cups vegetable juice
1¼ tsp. lemon juice

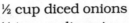

½ cup diced onions
½ tsp. garlic, minced
⅛ tsp. pepper

Preheat oven to 375°F. Rinse fillets and pat dry; place in a shallow baking dish. In a saucepan, combine remaining ingredients and bring to a boil. Pour sauce over fish and bake for 20 to 25 minutes. Occasionally baste.

Per serving
125 calories
8 mg cholesterol
300 mg sodium
0.012 gm saturated fat
0.03 gm fat

Exchanges per serving
2 meat
1 vegetable

On the side Cherry tomatoes with basil are really tasty with this pleasant seafood main dish. A ½ cup serving of white rice, or a slice of your favorite bread, a glass of no-fat milk, and a fresh fruit as dessert make the meal complete nutritionally.

Baked Whole Fish

1 (2 lb.) whole fish flounder
2½ Tbsp. vegetable oil
⅛ tsp. salt
⅛ tsp. paprika
½ tsp. lemon pepper
1 tsp. dried parsley flakes, crushed
¼ cup chopped green onions
2 Tbsp. margarine
1½ Tbsp. lemon juice

Preheat oven to 350°F. Wash and dry fish. Coat with the oil and season with salt, paprika, and lemon pepper. Bake 10 to 15 minutes. Combine parsley, onions, margarine, and lemon juice and spread over cooked fish. Place fish under broiler and broil until lightly brown.

Per serving
285 calories
10 mg cholesterol
269 mg sodium
2.0 gm saturated fat
15.0 gm fat

Exchanges per serving
1 fat
3 meat

On the side Long-grain wild rice, mixed vegetable of broccoli and cauliflower, steamed just until tender, and fresh berries, a half banana and a ½ cup of yogurt, well mixed in a blender, for a frothy dessert mousse make this meal nutritionally balanced.

Serves 2

¾ lb. sole fillets
⅛ tsp. salt
⅛ tsp. lemon pepper
⅛ tsp. lemon juice
2 Tbsp. dry white wine
1 tsp. margarine
1 tsp. minced garlic
3 Tbsp. herb-seasoned bread crumbs
1 tsp. dried parsley flakes

Lay fillets in a baking dish. Season with salt, lemon pepper, and lemon juice. Add wine. Place fish under broiler while preparing the bread crumbs. In skillet, melt margarine. Stir in the garlic and heat for about one minute. Add bread crumbs, stir until golden. Remove from heat and stir in parsley. When fish flakes easily, spread bread crumbs over fish. Return to broiler until crumbs are lightly browned. Serve with juices poured over fish.

Per serving
214 calories
18 mg cholesterol
339 mg sodium
0.5 gm saturated fat
3.3 gm fat

Exchanges per serving
1 fat
3 meat

On the side Carrots, steamed just until tender, are a colorful and healthful side dish for this great-tasting fish entree. Add a slice of bread, a glass of milk, and a melange of cantaloupe and honeydew melon balls for dessert and the meal is nutritionally complete.

Crunchy Fish Fillets

4 sole fillets

1½ cups herb-seasoned bread crumbs, crushed

3 Tbsp. dry white wine

1 tsp. dried parsley flakes, crushed

4 tsp. margarine

Preheat oven to 350°F. Lay fillets on nonstick baking pan. In bowl, mix bread crumbs, wine, and parsley. Cover fish with crumb mixture. Dot each fillet with 1 tsp. margarine. Bake 15 to 20 minutes.

Per serving
256 calories
0 mg cholesterol
376 mg sodium
1.0 gm saturated fat
6.1 gm fat

Exchanges per serving
½ bread
1 fat
2 meat

On the side Cook up some new potatoes with rosemary, toss together a salad of your favorite vegetables, pour a cold glass of nonfat milk, and choose your favorite fresh fruit for dessert, and this meal is nutritionally complete.

1 10 oz. pkg frozen spinach, thawed
2 tsp. minced onion
2 Tbsp. chopped green onion
½ tsp. nutmeg

⅛ tsp. salt
4 slices (3 oz. each) fillet of flounder
1 Tbsp. lemon juice
⅛ tsp. paprika

Preheat oven to 350°F. Combine spinach, onion, green onions, nutmeg, and salt. Lay fillets flat on a work surface. Spread a thin layer of spinach mixture over the top surface of fillets. Roll up and fasten with toothpick, if necessary. Place in a nonstick baking pan. Sprinkle with lemon juice and paprika. Bake for 20 to 25 minutes.

Per serving
135 calories
57 mg cholesterol
162 mg sodium
0.3 gm saturated fat
1.29 gm fat

Exchanges per serving
2 meat
1 vegetable

On the side A side order of rice and a dessert of mixed berries with nonfat vanilla yogurt make this meal complete nutritionally, appetizing to the eye, and delicious.

1 cup water
1½ cups chopped carrots
¼ tsp. salt
1 lb. fresh flounder fillets

Sauce:
½ cup margarine
1½ Tbsp. minced garlic
1½ Tbsp. lemon juice
1 cup sliced fresh mushrooms

In skillet, combine water, carrots, and salt; bring to a boil. Arrange fish over vegetable. Cover and simmer 8 to 10 minutes or until fish flakes easily. Lift fish and carrots out of water; keep warm. In saucepan, melt margarine. Sauté garlic. Stir in lemon juice and mushrooms; heat thoroughly. Serve over fish and carrots.

Per serving
180 calories
40 mg cholesterol
268 mg sodium
0 gm saturated fat
0.66 gm fat

Exchanges per serving
1 fat
3 meat
1 vegetable

On the side White rice is lovely with this tasty seafood main course. A dessert of baked apples with a glass of milk or some nonfat yogurt make the meal balanced nutritionally.

12 oz. sole or flounder fillets

2 tsp. ground ginger

2 Tbsp. oyster sauce

2 Tbsp. dry vermouth

1 tsp. sugar

1 tsp. soy sauce

Preheat oven to 375°F. Wash fish and cut each piece in half; place in shallow baking dish. Combine ginger, oyster sauce, vermouth, sugar and soy sauce. Pour over fish and bake. Bake for 20 to 25 minutes or until fish is flaky.

Per serving
183 calories
35 mg cholesterol
560 mg sodium
0.1 gm saturated fat
1.0 gm fat

Exchanges per serving
3½ meat

On the side Steamed carrots, ½ cup of white rice with saffron, and peaches with cream (nonfat yogurt cleverly disguised, of course), and this meal is nutritionally complete.

Oven Fish Fry

2 Tbsp. margarine, melted
1 Tbsp. lemon juice
⅛ tsp. pepper
⅛ tsp. paprika
¼ tsp. basil
⅛ tsp. garlic powder
1 lb. fillet of flounder
¼ cup dry whole-wheat bread crumbs

Preheat oven to 475°F. Combine margarine, lemon juice, pepper, paprika, basil, and garlic. Dredge fish in margarine-herb mixture and roll in bread crumbs. In a shallow baking dish, arrange fish. Spoon remaining margarine mixture over fish. Bake for 15 minutes or until fish flakes.

Per serving
208 calories
131 mg cholesterol
211 mg sodium
1.3 gm saturated fat
7.3 gm fat

Exchanges per serving
1 fat
3 meat

On the side Julienned zucchini strips mixed with carrots and stir-fried with a little margarine provide a colorful addition to this main fish dish. A serving of white rice, or a slice of bread, some fruit and a glass of milk round out the meal nutritionally.

6 small flounder fillets (2 to 3 oz. each)

⅓ cup minced onion

¼ cup light mayonnaise

¼ tsp. paprika

2 Tbsp. lime juice

⅛ tsp. pepper

⅛ tsp. salt

⅔ cup Parmesan cheese, grated

Preheat oven to 375°F. In a bowl, mix onion, mayonnaise, paprika, lime juice, salt, pepper, and Parmesan cheese. Spread mixture on fillets. Bake for 15 to 20 minutes or until brown.

Per serving
135 calories
14.5 mg cholesterol
198 mg sodium
2.4 gm saturated fat
5.1 gm fat

Exchanges per serving
1 fat
2 meat

On the side New potatoes with basil, a tossed salad, and a fruity milk shake make this meal nutritionally complete.

Ricotta Sole

⅔ cup low-fat ricotta cheese
1 Tbsp. Romano cheese
⅛ cup green onions, sliced
¼ tsp. dried basil
⅛ tsp. oregano
4 skinless sole fillets (3 oz. each)
⅔ cup spaghetti sauce
½ cup sliced mushrooms
⅓ cup part-skim shredded mozzarella

Preheat oven to 375°F. In bowl, combine ricotta cheese, romano cheese, green onion, basil, and oregano. Place about 2 tablespoons of cheese mixture on one end of each fillet. Roll fillets around cheese mixture; secure with wooden toothpicks. Place in a baking dish and bake for 20 to 25 minutes. Drain liquid off and spoon spaghetti sauce and mushrooms over fish rolls. Sprinkle with mozzarella cheese. Bake for 5 to 10 minutes more. Discard toothpicks before serving.

Per serving
261 calories
43 mg cholesterol
446 mg sodium
4.5 gm saturated fat
9.0 gm fat

Exchanges per serving
1 fat
3 meat
1 vegetable

On the side This dish looks and taste great with green noodles. Make a dessert dish of melon balls and strawberries with yogurt, and the meal is nutritionally complete.

175 Sole with Wine

3 Tbsp. margarine, melted
4 3 oz. sole fillets
½ cup dry white wine
1 Tbsp. lemon juice
1 tsp. dried parsley flakes
1 tsp. dried dillweed
⅛ tsp. thyme
¼ cup chopped green onion

Preheat oven to 350°F. Rinse fillets and pat dry. With melted margarine, baste fillets. Place fillets in 13 x 9-inch baking dish. Pour remaining margarine over fillets. Pour wine and lemon juice over fish. Sprinkle fish with remaining ingredients. Bake for about 10 minutes; check. The fish is done as soon as it is opaque and fairly firm to touch.

Per serving
189 calories
27 mg cholesterol
106 mg sodium
1.75 gm saturated fat
9.0 gm fat

Exchanges per serving
½ bread
2 meat

On the side Try brussel sprouts, steamed just until tender. They are always good with fish. Round this meal out nutritionally by adding a glass of milk and your favorite fruit for dessert.

Fort Snelling Fish Fillets

2 Tbsp. margarine
2 Tbsp. flour
1 tsp. salt
¼ tsp. nutmeg
½ tsp. dry mustard
1¼ cup skim milk
1 tsp. lemon juice
½ cup shredded part-skim cheddar cheese
Nonstick cooking spray
2 lbs. perch fillets

Preheat oven to 350°F. In saucepan, melt margarine over low heat. Stir in flour, salt, nutmeg, and mustard until smooth. Gradually stir in milk until thickened. Add lemon juice and cheese; stir until cheese melts.Spray a 13 x 9-inch baking pan with nonstick cooking spray. Place fish in pan and pour sauce over fish. Bake uncovered for 50 minutes.

Per serving
262 calories
180 mg cholesterol
595 mg sodium
2.0 gm saturated fat
7.2 gm fat

Exchanges per serving
1 fat
4 meat
½ skim milk

On the side Long-grain wild rice, a tossed salad, milk and fruit complete this meal nutritionally.

1 lb. sea perch
⅓ cup white wine

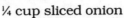

    ¼ cup sliced onion
    ¼ cup sliced green onion
    ⅛ tsp. lemon pepper
    1 tsp. minced garlic
    ⅛ tsp. dried tarragon
½ tsp. dried thyme
¼ tsp. basil
1 tomato, sliced

Place all ingredients into a bowl and marinate for 1 hour. Place fish and marinade into a baking dish and bake for 25 minutes at 350°F.

Per serving
184 calories
141 mg cholesterol
98 mg sodium
0.35 gm saturated fat
1.4 gm fat

Exchanges per serving
3 meat

On the side Colorful steamed carrots and a serving of white rice make the plate pleasing to the eye and the palate. Mix up a fruit and yogurt dessert and the meal is complete nutritionally.

Creamy Salmon Dish

Serves 6 **178**

1 15½-oz. can salmon in spring water
1½ tsp. margarine
½ cup diced celery
½ cup diced green pepper
1 tsp. minced onion
1¼ cup skim milk
1¼ Tbsp. cornstarch
¾ tsp. dillweed
1 cup frozen peas
3 hard-boiled eggs, sliced

Preheat oven to 375°F. Drain salmon. In a saucepan, melt margarine. Add celery, green pepper, and onion; cook until tender. Stir in milk. When hot, add cornstarch and stir constantly until mixture thickens. Season with dillweed. In a 1½ quart casserole dish, arrange half the peas, half the egg slices, and half the salmon. Repeat. Pour sauce over top. Cover and bake for 25 minutes.

Per serving
232 calories
128 mg cholesterol
143 mg sodium
1.25 gm saturated fat
4.5 gm fat

Exchanges per serving
½ bread
1 fat
2 meat

On the side Toss together a salad of fresh, colorful veggies, and choose your favorite fresh berries with yogurt for dessert and this meal is nutritionally complete.

179 Salmon Loaf

Serves 8

1 15½-oz. can salmon in spring water, drained
1¼ cups whole-wheat bread crumbs
1¼ cups cooked rice
1 egg, slightly beaten
¾ cup skim milk
½ cup chopped onion
1½ Tbsp. lemon juice
½ tsp. dried dillweed
⅛ tsp. ground pepper

Preheat oven to 375°F. In large bowl, combine all
ingredients; mix well. Put in 9 x 15-inch nonstick loaf
pan. Press down lightly. Bake 45 to 50 minutes or
until knife comes out clean.

Per serving
240 calories
63 mg cholesterol
230 mg sodium
0.93 gm saturated fat
5.0 gm fat

Exchanges per serving
1½ bread
1 meat

On the side Asparagus as a side dish to this wholesome salmon
loaf provides a nutritious and delicious addition to the meal.
Create a dessert of mixed melon slices and serve the meal with
a glass of cold nonfat milk for complete nutritional balance.

Salmon with Fruit

1 Tbsp. margarine
1 apple, cut into thin slices
1 pear, cut into thin slices
¼ cup raisins
2 Tbsp. lime juice
⅛ tsp. black pepper
12 oz. salmon fillets

Heat margarine in skillet and add apples, pears, raisins, and lime juice. Season with pepper. Sauté until fruit begins to soften. Place fish on broiler pan and broil on both sides until browned. Pour fruit mixture over salmon.

Per serving
349 calories
30 mg cholesterol
1118 mg sodium
2.2 gm saturated fat
12.0 gm fat

Exchanges per serving
1 fat
2½ fruit
3½ meat

On the side A raw cabbage salad and a dessert of white rice with milk and cinnamon make this meal nutritionally complete.

1 cup chopped onion
1 9-oz. package frozen green beans, thawed
¾ cup water
1½ Tbsp. soy sauce
½ Tbsp. Worcestershire sauce
1 Tbsp. cornstarch
¼ tsp. dry mustard
¼ tsp. lemon juice
1 15-oz. can salmon in water
1 8-oz. can bamboo shoots

In skillet, cook onions and green beans in ¼ cup water for about 5 to 10 minutes. In a bowl, combine soy sauce, Worcestershire sauce, cornstarch, mustard, lemon juice, and ¾ cup water; mix and set aside. Drain salmon and bamboo shoots. Stir cornstarch mixture in to vegetable mixture in skillet and cook until thickened. Stir in salmon and bamboo shoots. Cover and simmer for 10 minutes.

Per serving
191 calories
37.5 mg cholesterol
723 mg sodium
1.25 gm saturated fat
6.25 gm fat

Exchanges per serving
3 meat
1 vegetable

On the side Brown rice looks and tastes just right with this salmon entrée. A fruity yogurt dessert completes the meal nutritionally.

Teriyaki Salmon

1 lb. salmon fillets
¾ cup soy sauce
⅓ cup sherry
1¼ Tbsp. brown sugar
¼ tsp. ground ginger
1 tsp. minced garlic
1 tsp. Worcestershire sauce
2 Tbsp. lemon juice

Mix together all ingredients, except salmon; blend well. Place fish in a large plastic storage bag and put marinade in bag to cover salmon. Marinate in refrigerator for 2½ hours. Drain and broil on each side until done.

Per serving
150 calories
63 mg cholesterol
2546 mg sodium
1.06 gm saturated fat
7.2 gm fat

Exchanges per serving
3 meat

On the side Broccoli florets, gently steamed, a slice of bread and a glass of milk, and a baked apple dessert make this meal nutritionally complete.

183 Yogurt Salmon

1 lb. salmon fillet, skinned and boned
1 10-oz. package frozen spinach, thawed
1 cup chopped onion
¾ cup low-fat yogurt
2 tsp. Dijon-style mustard
2 tsp. honey
½ tsp. dried dill
2 Tbsp. lime juice

Preheat oven to 350°F. Rinse salmon and pat dry. Put spinach and onion in a baking dish. Place salmon on top of spinach and onion. Blend yogurt, mustard, honey, dill and lime juice; spread over salmon. Bake for 25 minutes or until fish is flaky.

Per serving
231 calories
65 mg cholesterol
92 mg sodium
1.5 gm saturated fat
8.4 gm fat

Exchanges per serving
3 meat
½ milk
1 vegetable

On the side Rice and fresh pears complete this meal complete nutritionally.

Scallops

Serves 4 **184**

1½ lb. scallops
2 Tbsp. margarine
2 Tbsp. lemon juice
1 Tbsp. soy sauce
⅛ cup cooking sherry
1 tsp. dried dillweed

Rinse scallops and pat dry. In skillet, melt margarine; add scallops and sauté. Add lemon juice, soy sauce, sherry and dill. Cover and simmer until scallops are done.

Per serving
222.5 calories
56 mg cholesterol
529 mg sodium
3.1 gm saturated fat
6.7 gm fat

Exchanges per serving
1 fat
4 meat

On the side Fresh sliced tomatoes, white rice with saffron, and honeydew melon slices add color and nutritionally complete this meal

Seafood & Fish ■ 195

2½ lbs. scallops
2 cucumbers, cut into 1-inch pieces
⅓ cup vegetable oil
2 Tbsp. lemon juice
1 bay leaf, crushed
⅛ tsp. garlic powder

Thread scallops and cucumbers alternately on each of 6 skewers. Mix together oil, lemon juice, bay leaf and garlic powder. Brush each serving with the mixture. Broil kabobs for 5 to 10 minutes, turning and basting frequently.

Per serving
231 calories
56 mg cholesterol
274 mg sodium
1.1 gm saturated fat
10.3 gm fat

Exchanges per serving
1 fat
4 meat
1 vegetable

On the side Rice looks and tastes great with these Scallops and Cucumber Kabobs. Fruit and yogurt complete the meal nutritionally.

Scallops in Garlic Sauce

1 lb. scallops
4 Tbsp. margarine
1½ tsp. garlic, minced
⅛ tsp. salt
⅛ tsp. lemon pepper
⅛ tsp. paprika

In saucepan, heat margarine and garlic on low heat.
Add scallops and cook 5 to 10 minutes or until done.
Season with salt, lemon pepper, and paprika. Serve.

Per serving
199 calories
37 mg cholesterol
391 mg sodium
2.0 gm saturated fat
12 gm fat

Exchanges per serving
1 fat
3 meat

On the side Zucchini squash, cut in julienne strips and sautéed
in a little margarine, a slice of bread or a serving of white rice,
and a fruit compote with yogurt for dessert complete this meal
deliciously and nutritiously.

1 Tbsp. vegetable oil
1 cup chopped onion
1 tsp. minced garlic
2 cups sliced mushrooms
4 Tbsp. tomato paste
¼ cup dry white wine
1 tsp. dried parsley flakes
1½ tsp. dried oregano
1 can (28 oz.) plum tomatoes
1 lb. sea scallops

In a saucepan, heat oil. Add onion, garlic and mushrooms; cook until tender. Add remaining ingredients, except scallops. Bring to a boil. Reduce heat and simmer for 30 minutes. Add scallops and cook for 5 to 10 minutes.

Per serving
224 calories
37 mg cholesterol
469 mg sodium
0.55 gm saturated fat
4.4 gm fat

Exchanges per serving
1 fat
3 meat
1 vegetable

On the side White rice is perfect with this scallop dish and provides the bread exchange for this meal. Add a glass of milk and fruit for dessert and you've got all the makings for a nutritionally complete meal.

Scallops with Tomato-Garlic Sauce

Serves 4 **188**

1 tsp. vegetable oil
2 tsp. minced garlic
1 lb. scallops, rinsed
1 Tbsp. cornstarch
1 cup sliced mushrooms
1 tomato, chopped
¼ cup green onions
1 tsp. dried parsley flakes, crushed
½ tsp. oregano
¼ cup dry vermouth
1½ Tbsp. lemon juice

In a skillet, add oil and garlic. Sauté for a couple of minutes. Add scallops; cook until opaque. Remove and keep warm. Add cornstarch to juices in pan; mix over medium heat until thickened. Add mushrooms, tomatoes, onions, parsley, and oregano. Cook 3 to 4 minutes. Add vermouth and lemon juice; cook for 2 to 3 minutes. Pour sauce over scallops.

Per serving
180 calories
24.5 mg cholesterol
186 mg sodium
0.38 gm saturated fat
2.25 gm fat

Exchanges per serving
3 meat
1 vegetable

On the side Rice is a nice side dish with this tasty fish dish. Create a dessert of berries and fruit with yogurt and the meal is nutritionally balanced and delicious.

189 Baked Shrimp

12 raw jumbo shrimp, shelled and deveined
½ cup melted margarine
1 cup dry bread crumbs
1 tsp. dried parsley flakes
1 Tbsp. finely chopped fresh dill
¼ cup dry white wine
⅛ tsp. pepper
1 tsp. celery seeds

Preheat oven to 350°F. With a sharp knife, split shrimp in half, being careful not to cut all the way through; set aside. Combine margarine and remaining ingredients; mix well. Stuff each shrimp with about 2 tablespoons of the mixture. Place in baking dish. Bake at 350°F for 20 minutes.

Per serving
235 calories
130 mg cholesterol
215 mg sodium
1.3 gm saturated fat
8.8 gm fat

Exchanges per serving
1 bread
1½ fat
3 meat

On the side Cherry tomatoes with basil are delicious with this succulent shrimp dish. A dessert of mixed strawberries and bananas with yogurt makes the meal nutritionally complete.

Broiled Shrimp and Scallops

¼ cup vegetable oil
½ cup low-sodium tomato sauce
¼ cup soy sauce
1 Tbsp. lime juice
½ tsp. lemon pepper
1 tsp. minced garlic
1 Tbsp. minced onion
1 lb. large shrimp, peeled and deveined
1 lb. scallops

Combine all ingredients, except shrimp and scallops; mix well. In a shallow pan, place shrimp and scallops and pour marinade over. Marinate for 1 hour. Place seafood on broiler pan and broil; turn and brush with marinade.

Per serving
209 calories
145 mg cholesterol
550 mg sodium
1.4 gm saturated fat
10.0 gm fat

Exchanges per serving
2 fat
3 meat

On the side Zucchini, cut julienne and stir-fried, is really tasty with this marinated seafood entree. A side order of rice, a glass of milk, and fruit for dessert make the meal complete nutritionally.

3 Tbsp. margarine
16 uncooked large shrimp, peeled and deveined
2 tsp. coriander seeds, crushed
⅛ tsp. salt
⅛ tsp. pepper
⅛ tsp. paprika
3 Tbsp. white wine

In a skillet, melt margarine, add shrimp, coriander, salt, pepper and paprika; stir until shrimp are opaque. Add wine and bring to a boil. Serve.

Per serving
218 calories
130 mg. cholesterol
177 mg sodium
1.2 gm saturated fat
9.0 gm fat

Exchanges per serving
1 fat
3 meat

On the side Snow pea pods, simply sautéed, are a delightful accompaniment to Coriander Shrimp. Rice, in ½ cup per person servings, and mixed fruit salad for dessert complete the meal nutritionally.

Creole Shrimp

Serves 6   **192**

2 Tbsp. margarine
1 cup chopped onions
1 cup chopped green pepper
¾ cup chopped celery
1 tsp. minced garlic
1 tsp. thyme
1 cup low-sodium chicken broth
1 Tbsp. flour
3 cups chopped tomatoes
1 tsp. chili powder
⅛ tsp. Tabasco sauce
2 lbs. raw shrimp, shelled and deveined

In a skillet, melt margarine; add onions, green
peppers, celery, garlic and thyme until tender. Add
chicken broth and blend in flour, stirring constantly.
Add remaining ingredients, except shrimp; simmer 20
minutes. Add shrimp and cook for 10 minutes or until
shrimp is done.

Per serving
257 calories
260 mg cholesterol
312 mg sodium
1.3 gm saturated fat
4.0 gm fat

Exchanges per serving
½ bread
1 fat
3 meat

On the side New potatoes with skins on, boiled, then sautéed
whole in a little margarine, are very nice beside this New
Orleans-style main dish. Try a mixed fruit salad of celery,
apples, and raisins with yogurt to complete the meal.

2 Tbsp. margarine
¾ cup diced onions
¾ cup diced green pepper
1 apple, peeled, cored and chopped fine
1 tsp. curry powder
1 16-oz. can low-sodium tomatoes
1 lb. raw shrimp, peeled and deveined
⅛ tsp. lemon pepper

In a skillet, melt margarine. Add onion, green pepper, apple, lemon pepper, and curry powder. Stir and cook until onion is tender. Add tomatoes. Break up tomatoes with fork as they cook. Add shrimp. Cover and simmer for 15 minutes or until shrimp is cooked through. Sprinkle with lemon pepper and serve.

Per serving
241 calories
173 mg cholesterol
259 mg sodium
1.4 gm saturated fat
8.5 gm fat

Exchanges per serving
1 fat
3 meat
1 vegetable

On the side Zucchini with diced tomatoes provides just the right taste to counterbalance the curry flavor of the shrimp. Serve this with pita slices or rice and a melange of exotic fruits to make the dinner an international experience.

Hot Shrimp

1 Tbsp. margarine
3 Tbsp. lemon juice
¼ tsp. salt
¼ tsp. liquid hot pepper sauce
1 lb. medium raw shrimp, shelled and
deveined
¼ tsp. dried parsley flakes

In skillet, melt margarine. Add lemon juice, salt, pepper sauce, and shrimp. Stirring occasionally, cook shrimp until shrimp turns pink. Sprinkle parsley on top of shrimp.

Per serving
110 calories
111 mg cholesterol
274 mg sodium
0.34 gm saturated fat
1.5 gm fat

Exchanges per serving
2 meat

On the side Cherry tomatoes with basil, a serving of rice, a glass of cold milk, and mixed melon balls for dessert make this meal nutritionally complete.

195 Seafood Casserole

Serves 4

1 can celery soup
1 cup skim milk
3 tsp. lime juice
⅛ tsp. pepper
⅛ tsp. salt
⅛ tsp. paprika
½ lb. shrimp
2 cups cooked rice
1 cup frozen peas, thawed
¼ cup grated Parmesan cheese

Preheat oven to 350°F. Cook soup, milk, lime juice, and seasoning, stirring until well blended. In a 1½ quart casserole dish, pour half of the soup mixture, then add alternate layers of shrimp, rice, and peas. Add the remaining soup. Sprinkle with cheese. Bake, covered, for 20 to 25 minutes.

Per serving
331 calories
81 mg cholesterol
1011 mg sodium
4.0 gm saturated fat
9.4 gm fat

Exchanges per serving
2 bread
2 meat

On the side A tossed salad with your favorite dressing, a glass of nonfat milk, and baked apple dessert make this meal nutritionally balanced.

Sesame Shrimp Broil

2 lb. uncooked medium shrimp, peeled and deveined
½ cup soy sauce
½ cup chopped green onions
¼ cup sesame oil
¼ cup water
2 Tbsp. minced garlic
2 tsp. ginger
¾ tsp. nutmeg
¼ tsp. cinnamon

Combine all ingredients in a large bowl. Cover and let marinate for several hours. Drain shrimp, discarding marinade. Thread shrimp on skewers. Broil 1 to 2 minutes on each side.

Per serving
200 calories
130 mg cholesterol
825 mg sodium
2.3 gm saturated fat
10.0 gm fat

Exchanges per serving
1 fat
3 meat

On the side New potatoes with rosemary are just right with this entrée. The servings of shrimp are large because nobody can eat just a little of this delicious dish. A mixed fruit salad with yogurt dressing completes the meal nutritionally.

8 oz. raw shrimp, peeled and deveined

2 Tbsp. margarine

2 tsp. sesame seeds

¼ cup chopped green onions

3 Tbsp. soy sauce

1 tsp. Worcestershire sauce

½ tsp. ginger

1 cup cooked rice

Cut shrimp into small pieces. In a skillet, heat margarine and sauté shrimp with sesame seeds until shrimp is done. Stir in onions, soy sauce, Worcestershire sauce, and ginger. Stir often. Serve over hot rice.

Per serving
318 calories
173 mg cholesterol
533 mg sodium
2.4 gm saturated fat
7.0 gm fat

Exchanges per serving
1 bread
½ fat
4 meat

On the side A serving of stir-fried snow pea pods is perfect beside this oriental-style entree. An orange, simply sectioned, is just right for dessert.

Shrimp Creole

Serves 2 **198**

2 Tbsp. margarine
¼ cup sliced mushrooms
⅛ cup chopped green onions
¼ cup chopped green pepper
½ tsp. minced garlic
1 8-oz. can low-sodium tomato sauce
1 cup cooked, small shrimp
1 cup cooked rice

In a skillet, heat margarine. Sauté mushrooms, green onions, green pepper, and garlic until crisp-tender. Stir in tomato sauce and shrimp. Simmer for 10 to 15 minutes. Serve over hot rice.

Per serving
349 calories
221 mg cholesterol
640 mg sodium
2.3 gm saturated fat
13.3 gm fat

Exchanges per serving
1 bread
1 fat
2 meat
1 vegetable

On the side This easy main dish meal is complete all by itself. A glass of milk and your choice of fruit make the meal nutritionally balanced.

Seafood & Fish ■ 209

1½ Tbsp. margarine

12 oz. fresh shrimp, peeled and deveined

2 tsp. minced garlic

2 tsp. sherry

1 tsp. dried parsley flakes, crushed

In a large skillet, heat margarine. Add shrimp and garlic. Cook and stir frequently until shrimp turns pink. Stir in sherry. Sprinkle with parsley flakes.

Per serving
*195 calories
130 mg cholesterol
178 mg sodium
1.05 gm saturated fat
6.0 gm fat*

Exchanges per serving
*1 fat
3 meat*

On the side Steamed green beans and white rice go well with this variation of the basic shrimp entrée. A mixed fruit salad with yogurt make the meal complete nutritionally.

Shrimp Kabob

6 Tbsp. lemon juice

4 tsp. soy sauce

20 oz. shrimp, shelled and deveined

2 medium tomatoes, cut into wedges

1 medium green pepper, cut into larger
    chunks

1 small onion, cut into wedges

In small bowl, combine lemon juice and soy sauce;
add shrimp and coat. On a skewer, thread shrimp,
tomato wedges, pepper squares and onion wedges.
Alternate ingredients. Broil, turning and basting with
reserve marinade until shrimp is firm.

Per serving
163 calories
130 mg cholesterol
825 mg sodium
0.23 gm saturated fat
1.0 gm fat

Exchanges per serving
2½ meat
1 vegetable

On the side These colorful kabobs look great over a bed of white
rice, and the rice helps to balance the meal. Add a glass of
milk and some fresh mixed fruits for dessert for nutritional
completeness.

1 Tbsp. vegetable oil
2 lbs. shrimp, peeled and deveined
    ¼ cup green onions, sliced
    ⅓ cup chicken broth, low-sodium
    1½ cups frozen peas, thawed
    3 Tbsp. soy sauce
    ½ tsp. ground ginger
1 Tbsp. sherry
2 tsp. cornstarch
1 Tbsp. water

This is a LOW FAT DISH

In a skillet, heat oil, add shrimp and green onions, and cook until shrimp turns pink. Add chicken broth, peas, and ginger. Cook until peas are tender. Stir in sherry and cornstarch dissolved in water. Cook until thickened.

Per serving
321 calories
222 mg cholesterol
330 mg sodium
0.3 gm saturated fat
2.3 gm fat

Exchanges per serving
1 bread
3 meat

On the side White rice is always right with oriental-style cooking. A mixed vegetable, stir-fried, goes well with this dish also. These plus a glass of milk and your favorite fruit for dessert make the meal complete nutritionally.

Shrimp Scampi

24 oz. shelled and deveined jumbo shrimp
4 Tbsp. flour
1 Tbsp. minced garlic
2 Tbsp. vegetable oil
¼ cup dry white wine
1 Tbsp. lemon juice
⅛ tsp. pepper

Dip shrimp in flour. In skillet, sauté garlic in vegetable oil until lightly browned. Add shrimp and sauté until shrimp turns pink. Add wine and bring to a boil. Stir in lemon juice and pepper. Serve.

Per serving
185 calories
130 mg cholesterol
2 mg sodium
0.33 gm saturated fat
7.0 gm fat

Exchanges per serving
½ bread
2 meat

On the side Green noodles go well with this version of traditional scampi and they offer a nice alternative to rice. A mixed green salad, a glass of milk, and a fruit for dessert make the meal complete nutritionally.

4 red snapper fillets
½ cup dry white wine
    1 cup water
    1 cup sliced carrots

    1 cup sliced celery
    ⅓ cup green onions, chopped
    ½ tsp. dried thyme
1 bay leaf
⅛ tsp. pepper

In skillet, add all ingredients, except fish, and bring to a boil. Reduce heat and simmer for 15 minutes. Place fish on a rack and lower into broth. Bring to a boil, cover, and simmer for 5 minutes. Serve.

Per serving
178 calories
31 mg cholesterol
96 mg sodium
0.2 gm saturated fat
1.1 gm fat

Exchanges per serving
3 meat

On the side Brown rice is perfect with this poached snapper recipe. A salad of cabbage, carrots, and lettuce with your favorite dressing plus a fruit with yogurt dessert make this meal nutritionally complete.

4 6-oz. red snapper fillets
1 Tbsp. lemon juice
1 Tbsp. vegetable oil
⅔ cup chopped green pepper
⅔ cup chopped onions
2 Tbsp. white wine
1 tsp. dried parsley flakes
½ tsp. cayenne pepper
1 cup chopped tomatoes
2 Tbsp. grated Parmesan cheese
⅛ tsp. Tabasco sauce

Preheat oven to 350°F. Sprinkle fish with lemon juice. In skillet, heat oil, stir in green pepper and onions, and cook until tender. Add fish and cook about a minute on each side. Add wine, parsley, cayenne, and simmer for 5 minutes. Transfer to baking dish. Spoon tomatoes over fish. Sprinkle with cheese and Tabasco sauce. Bake about 8 to 10 minutes.

Per serving
340 calories
43 mg cholesterol
115 mg sodium
3.25 gm saturated fat
8.0 gm fat

Exchanges per serving
6 meat

On the side Asparagus, steamed just until tender, a small baked potato, a glass of milk and your favorite fresh fruit for dessert make this meal nutritionally complete.

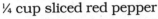

¼ cup sliced green onions
¼ cup sliced green pepper
   ¼ cup sliced red pepper
   1 cup sliced fresh mushrooms
   ⅛ tsp. lemon pepper
   1 lb. snapper
   1 dozen green beans, washed and cut in half
½ tsp. lemon juice
¼ tsp. dried tarragon

Preheat oven to 350°F. In bottom of a baking dish, place onions, green peppers, red peppers, and mushrooms. Sprinkle with lemon pepper. Lay fish on top of vegetables. Place green beans on top of fish. Sprinkle with lemon juice and tarragon. Cover and bake for 25 minutes.

Per serving
178 calories
55 mg cholesterol
105 mg sodium
0.35 gm saturated fat
1.9 gm fat

Exchanges per serving
3 meat
1 vegetable

On the side White rice or a small baked potato add the starch course, and a glass of milk and a fresh fruit for dessert make the meal complete nutritionally.

Baked Fish with Sour Cream

1 small onion, sliced thin
⅔ cup dry white wine
2 Tbsp. lemon juice
6 swordfish fillets (approx. 3 oz. ea.)
⅛ tsp. salt
½ tsp. lemon pepper
1 cup light sour cream

Preheat oven to 400°F. Cover the bottom of a baking dish with onions. Add wine and lemon juice; stir. Bake for 10 minutes. Arrange fish fillets over onions. Sprinkle with salt and lemon pepper. Bake for an additional 15 minutes covered. Uncover and spread sour cream over fish and broil until cream is lightly brown. Serve.

Per serving
240 calories
66 mg cholesterol
383 mg sodium
2.3 gm saturated fat
8.3 gm fat

Exchanges per serving
1 fat
3 meat

On the side Long-grain wild rice is just right with this robust fish dish. A side salad of mixed greens and a fresh pear, sliced and placed attractively on a glass plate with a slight sprinkle of nutmeg, for dessert complete the meal. Remember adding a glass of milk makes this meal complete.

1 lb. swordfish
¼ cup vegetable oil
2 Tbsp. red wine vinegar
1 tsp. garlic powder
2 tsp. Dijon-style mustard
½ tsp. dried basil
⅓ cup chopped onions
1 bay leaf

Combine all ingredients in a shallow dish. Coat swordfish with marinade and let stand at least 1 hour, turning occasionally. Place swordfish on broiling pan and broil on each side, basting occasionally.

Per serving
255 calories
43 mg cholesterol
65 mg sodium
3.5 gm saturated fat
10.0 gm fat

Exchanges per serving
1 fat
4 meat

On the side White rice and brussel sprouts go very well with this marinated fish dish. Top off with a melange of fruits and berries with yogurt dressing and the meal is nutritionally complete.

Swordfish with Mustard Sauce

Serves 4 **208**

1½ lb. swordfish
1½ Tbsp. lemon juice
2½ Tbsp. light mayonnaise
5 Tbsp. low-fat yogurt
1½ Tbsp. Dijon-style mustard
1½ tsp. dried tarragon

Heat broiler. Cook fish on one side. Pour 1 tablespoon lemon juice over fish. While fish is cooking, combine remaining ingredients; mix well. Cook fish for 1 to 2 minutes on other side, then pour sauce over fish. Continue to cook fish until done.

Per serving
193 calories
56 mg cholesterol
144 mg sodium
2.0 gm saturated fat
7.1 gm fat

Exchanges per serving
1 fat
3 meat

On the side A simple baked potato is always good with swordfish. Asparagus spears, steamed just until tender, a glass of milk and you choice of fruit for dessert and the meal is nutritionally complete.

209 Swordfish Steaks

4 swordfish steaks
2 Tbsp. soy sauce
1 tsp. Worcestershire sauce
3 Tbsp. dry white wine
3 Tbsp. lemon juice
1 tsp. minced garlic
½ tsp. lemon pepper

Place swordfish on broiling pan. Combine remaining ingredients. Baste swordfish with marinade and broil until fish is done; baste several times while broiling.

Per serving
160 calories
33 mg cholesterol
549 mg sodium
0.9 gm saturated fat
3.4 gm fat

Exchanges per serving
3 meat

On the side Fresh cooked corn on the cob tastes great with this broiled fish. A tossed salad of mixed greens with your favorite dressing, a glass of nonfat milk, and melon slices for dessert make the meal complete nutritionally.

Bread Crumb Fillets

2 Tbsp. margarine, melted
¼ cup minced onion
1 Tbsp. lemon juice
1 Tbsp. minced garlic
1 tsp. oregano
⅛ tsp. ground pepper
⅛ tsp. lemon pepper
4 trout fillets
½ tsp. paprika
¼ cup whole-wheat bread crumbs

Combine margarine, onion, lemon juice, garlic, oregano, ground pepper, lemon pepper, and mix well. Spoon an equal amount of mixture over each fillet. Sprinkle with paprika; top with bread crumbs. Spray broiler rack with nonstick cooking spray. Place fish on rack. Broil 3 to 4 inches away from heat. Broil until topping is lightly browned and fish flakes easily.

Per serving
254 calories
48 mg cholesterol
139 mg sodium
1.2 gm saturated fat
8.9 gm fat

Exchanges per serving
½ bread
1 fat
3 meat

On the side Steamed spinach looks and tastes great with this trout dish. Combine strawberries and nonfat milk in the blender and freeze the result for a refreshing mousse for dessert. This simple meal is nutritionally balanced.

2 Tbsp. vegetable oil
1 Tbsp. vinegar
1½ tsp. ground coriander
¾ tsp. minced garlic
½ tsp. dried parsley flakes
½ tsp. tarragon
1 tsp. oregano
4 trout fillets
2 cups coarsely chopped tomatoes

Beat together oil, vinegar, coriander, and garlic. Add parsley, tarragon and oregano, and mix. Stir in tomatoes. Place fish on broiler pan and brush lightly with oil. Broil fish until done. Pour dressing over fish and serve.

Per serving
178 calories
48 mg cholesterol
8.7 mg sodium
0.9 gm saturated fat
7.0 gm fat

Exchanges per serving
1 fat
2 meat

On the side A serving of green noodles, a tossed salad, a glass of milk, and a dessert of mixed melon balls make this meal nutritionally complete.

Marinated Trout

4 trout fillets
¾ cup soy sauce
¼ cup cooking sherry
1½ Tbsp. lime juice
1 tsp. ground cloves
½ cup vegetable oil

Rinse and pat fillets. In a bowl, mix all ingredients. Place fillets in shallow baking dish. Pour marinade over fish. Let stand for 1½ hours. Spray broiler pan with nonstick spray. Broil fish. Baste occasionally with marinade until fish is flaky.

Per serving
123 calories
27 mg cholesterol
1125 mg sodium
0.3 gm saturated fat
1.3 gm fat

Exchanges per serving
2 meat

On the side Green noodles, a slaw-style salad of cabbage and carrots, a glass of milk, and a baked apple make this meal nutritionally complete.

2 tsp. vegetable oil
2 Tbsp. minced onion
¼ cup chopped red pepper
1 tsp. minced garlic
¼ cup water
1 tsp. soy sauce
½ tsp. lemon juice
1 Tbsp. sugar
1 Tbsp. vinegar
⅛ tsp. ground pepper
1 tsp. flour, dissolved in 2 Tbsp. water
4 trout fillets

In skillet, heat oil. Add onions, red pepper, and garlic; cook until soft. Add water, soy sauce, lemon juice, sugar, vinegar, and ground pepper. Bring to a boil. Add fillets; cover and simmer until fish flakes easily. Transfer fillets to serving platter; keep warm. Add flour mixture to skillet. Cook, stirring constantly until thickened. Pour over fillets.

Per serving
172 calories
48 mg cholesterol
92.7 mg sodium
0.88 gm saturated fat
9.4 gm fat

Exchanges per serving
1 fat
3 meat

On the side A serving of white rice, a side dish of steamed cauliflower, and a dessert of fruity frozen pops complete this meal. Add a glass of milk for total nutritional balance.

Trout in Oatmeal

2 trout fillets
⅛ tsp. salt
⅛ tsp. lemon pepper
¼ cup fine oatmeal
2 Tbsp. margarine

Season fish with salt and lemon pepper. Coat both sides with oatmeal. Heat margarine in a skillet and sauté trout until cooked through and browned.

Per serving
250 calories
48 mg cholesterol
370 mg sodium
2.6 gm saturated fat
10.3 gm fat

Exchanges per serving
½ bread
1 fat
3 meat

On the side Freshly sliced cucumbers interspersed with tomato slices look attractive on the plate, taste delicious with this healthy trout dish, and provide the vegetable component needed to balance the meal. Make a drink of 1 cup of skim milk plus a cup of frozen peaches, mixed in the blender until thick and frothy, and this meal is nutritionally complete.

215 Creamed Tuna

¼ cup light mayonnaise
2 Tbsp. flour
1 cup skim milk
½ tsp. minced onion
¼ tsp. minced garlic
⅛ tsp. pepper
1 6⅛-oz. can tuna in spring water
1 cup frozen corn, thawed
¼ cup shredded part-skim cheddar cheese
2 whole-wheat English muffins

In saucepan, combine mayonnaise and flour. Gradually stir in milk, onion, garlic, and pepper. Cook over low heat until mixture boils, stirring constantly. Add tuna, corn and cheese. Heat until cheese melts. Serve open faced over whole-wheat English muffins.

Per serving
264 calories
28.9 mg cholesterol
521 mg sodium
1.1 gm saturated fat
7.0 gm fat

Exchanges per serving
1 bread
1 fat
2 meat

On the side Crunchy carrot and celery sticks and a strawberry freezer drink complete this meal nutritionally.

Peppered Tuna Dish

8 oz. macaroni
1¾ cup skim milk
3½ Tbsp. cornstarch
¼ cup water
¾ cup sliced fresh mushrooms
¾ tsp. thyme
½ tsp. pepper
1 cup chopped zucchini
1 6⅛-oz. can tuna in spring water
½ cup sliced radishes

Preheat oven to 375°F. Cook macaroni according to package directions; drain and set aside. In saucepan, heat milk. Add cornstarch and water to milk, stirring constantly until it thickens. Add mushrooms, thyme, and pepper. In a 2½ quart casserole dish, arrange macaroni in the bottom, top with zucchini, then place tuna with radishes on top. Pour sauce over the top layer. Cover and bake for 40 to 45 minutes or until zucchini is tender.

Per serving
157 calories
2.5 mg cholesterol
73 mg sodium
0 gm saturated fat
0.37 gm fat

Exchanges per serving
1 bread
1 meat
1 vegetable

On the side Make a drink of 1 cup of skim milk with 1 cup of frozen peaches and this meal is complete nutritionally.

1 7-oz. pkg. elbow macaroni
1 6⅛-oz. can tuna in spring water
1 Tbsp. margarine
¼ cup chopped onion
1 can cream of mushroom soup
¾ cup water
¼ cup shredded part-skim American cheese
1 tsp. dried parsley flakes

Cook macaroni according to package directions. Drain and flake tuna. In a large skillet, melt margarine. Sauté onions. Add soup, water, cheese, tuna, and parsley. Stir until cheese melts. Add macaroni and heat on low for about 10 minutes.

Per serving
190 calories
16 mg cholesterol
340 mg sodium
1.5 gm saturated fat
5.2 gm fat

Exchanges per serving
1 bread
1 fat
1 meat

On the side A tossed salad of mixed greens, a glass of milk, and an apple, baked with a little cinnamon on top, make this meal delicious and nutritionally complete.

Tuna Cakes

1 6⅛-oz. tuna in spring water, drained
½ cup crushed saltines
1 egg, beaten
⅓ cup skim milk
2 Tbsp. finely chopped onions
¼ tsp. Worcestershire sauce
⅛ tsp. pepper
¼ tsp. prepared mustard
1 Tbsp. margarine

In a bowl, combine all ingredients, except margarine. Shape into 6 patties. In a skillet, heat margarine; add patties and cook over medium heat. Cook and brown on both sides.

Per serving
284 calories
127 mg cholesterol
582 mg sodium
2.9 gm saturated fat
10.8 gm fat

Exchanges per serving
1 bread
3½ meat

On the side Steamed carrots are just right with these tasty tuna patties. They provide the vegetable component for this meal and they look smashing on the plate. A glass of milk and a dessert of mixed berries and melon balls provide the other components that complete the meal nutritionally complete.

1 cup noodles
1 cup skim milk
1 Tbsp. flour
1 6⅛-oz. can tuna in spring water, drained
¾ cup fresh mushrooms, sliced
1 Tbsp. minced onion
¼ cup finely chopped red pepper
1 tsp. dried parsley flakes
1 tsp. basil
1 tsp. celery seed
⅛ tsp. black pepper

Preheat oven to 325°F. Cook noodles in water until done; drain. In saucepan, add milk and flour; cook until thickened. In bowl, combine tuna, mushrooms, onions, red pepper, and seasonings; mix well. Add milk mixture; mix again. Stir in noodles. Fill baking dish with tuna mixture. Bake for 40 minutes.

Per serving
289 calories
83 mg cholesterol
114 mg sodium
0.05 gm saturated fat
3.7 gm fat

Exchanges per serving
1½ bread
1½ meat
1 vegetable

On the side A glass of milk and a fresh fruit for dessert are all you need to make this meal nutritionally complete.

Tuna Soufflé

2 6⅛-oz. cans tuna in spring water
½ cup bran cereal, uncooked
½ cup skim milk
2 Tbsp. minced onion
1 Tbsp. lime juice
1 Tbsp. dried parsley flakes
⅛ tsp. black pepper
1 tsp. celery seed
⅛ tsp. paprika
1 egg white

Heat oven to 325°F. Drain tuna and flake. In a large bowl, mix tuna, bran, milk, onion, lime juice, parsley, pepper, celery seed, and paprika. Beat egg white until stiff peak forms; fold into tuna mixture. Put into 1-quart baking dish. Bake for 40 minutes or until brown.

Per serving
139 calories
426 mg cholesterol
40 mg sodium
0.31 gm saturated fat
1.3 gm fat

Exchanges per serving
1 bread
1 meat

On the side Asparagus, gently steamed, is great with this soufflé. A frothy dessert of yogurt blended with pears and topped with cinnamon finishes the meal, refreshes the palate, and nutritionally balances this dinner.

4 tsp. vegetable oil

¾ cup sliced onions

¾ cup chopped tomatoes

¾ cup low-sodium tomato sauce

⅛ tsp. pepper

1 8-oz. can tuna in spring water, drained, flaked

⅛ tsp. hot sauce

4 corn tortillas

⅔ cup skim cheddar cheese, shredded

1 cup shredded lettuce

In skillet, heat oil; add onions and sauté for 5 minutes. Add tomatoes, tomato sauce, pepper, and hot sauce; cook for 5 minutes more. Stir in tuna and cook through. Fill each tortilla with ¼ each of tuna mixture, cheese, and lettuce.

Per serving
252 calories
18 mg cholesterol
136 mg sodium
4.5 gm saturated fat
10.8 gm fat

Exchanges per servings
1 bread
1 fat
2 meat

On the side A small dollop of cottage cheese with thin slices of avocado and a Mexican-style salad of cucumbers, tomatoes, celery, onions, and green and red peppers with oil-free dressing make this meal an international delight.

Baked Fish with Mushrooms

1 lb. walleye fillets
1½ Tbsp. margarine
2 cups fresh sliced mushrooms
⅔ cup sliced green onion
⅛ tsp. thyme
¼ tsp. dried crushed tarragon
⅛ tsp. paprika
1½ Tbsp. margarine

Preheat oven to 450°F. Arrange fish on a baking dish. In a skillet, heat margarine and cook mushrooms, onion, thyme and tarragon until tender. Spoon over fish. Sprinkle with paprika. Bake for 10 minutes or until fish flakes easily.

Per serving
164 calories
97 mg cholesterol
117 mg sodium
1.0 gm saturated fat
15.8 gm fat

Exchanges per serving
1 fat
3 meat
½ vegetable

On the side A serving of brown rice, a tossed salad, and a broiled grapefruit with cinnamon for dessert complete the meal. Add a glass of milk and the meal is nutritionally balanced.

1 lb. walleye
1 tsp. dried parsley flakes
½ tsp. salt
⅛ tsp. pepper
½ cup thinly sliced onions
1 small tomato, cut into thin slices
1 Tbsp. lemon juice
1 Tbsp. vegetable oil

Preheat oven to 375°F. Cut fillets into six servings. Arrange fish in baking dish into which the vegetable oil has been poured. Sprinkle with salt and pepper. Top with onion and tomato slices. Sprinkle with lemon juice and parsley. Cover and bake for 25 minutes or until fish flakes easily.

Per serving
124 calories
73 mg cholesterol
52 mg sodium
0.28 gm saturated fat
2.3 gm fat

Exchanges per serving
2 meat

On the side Brown rice works well with this festive-looking main dish. A salad of mixed greens and quick-to-fix applesauce from the blender complete the meal. Add a glass of milk and you have it all nutritionally.

Fish Florentine

2 tsp. margarine
¼ cup minced onion
1¾ cup skim milk
2 tsp. chicken bouillon powder
½ tsp. paprika
2 Tbsp. cornstarch
1 lb. walleye fillets
3 cups sliced potatoes
1 10 oz. package frozen spinach, thawed

Preheat oven to 375°F. In skillet, melt margarine. Add onions and cook until tender. Stir in the milk, bouillon, and paprika. Mix in cornstarch; stir constantly over medium heat until mixture thickens. Cut fillets into ½ inch slices. Arrange potatoes in 2½ quart casserole dish, top with spinach, then fish, then sauce. Cover and bake for 1½ hours or until potatoes are tender.

Per serving
335 calories
31 mg cholesterol
430 mg sodium
0.4 gm saturated fat
2.5 gm fat

Exchanges per serving
1½ bread
2 meat
½ skim milk
1 vegetable

On the side This hearty dish has it all: starch, protein, vegetable, milk. Add a dessert of mixed fruits and the meal is nutritionally complete.

2 tsp. oil
⅔ cup onions, chopped
1 tsp. minced garlic
1 cup chopped tomatoes
¾ tsp. dried basil
¼ tsp. oregano
1 tsp. dried parsley flakes
1½ Tbsp. lemon juice
8 oz. walleye fillet
⅛ tsp. pepper
⅛ tsp. salt
¼ cup water

In skillet, heat oil; add onion and garlic; sauté until golden. Stir in tomatoes, basil, oregano, parsley, and lemon juice. Sprinkle fish with salt and pepper. Lay fish on top of sauce in skillet. Add water; cover and steam fish for 10 minutes or until fish flakes easily.

Per serving
191 calories
97 mg cholesterol
210 mg sodium
0.8 gm saturated fat
5.8 gm fat

Exchanges per serving
1 fat
3 meat
1 vegetable

On the side Cook up a batch of fresh beets to accompany this updated version of a traditional French recipe. Mix mandarin orange slices, sliced strawberries, and seedless grapes and top with yogurt dressing for a healthy dessert that makes this meal nutritionally complete.

Orange Fried Fish Fillets

4 walleye fillets (approx. 3 oz. each)
½ cup frozen orange concentrate
⅛ tsp. lemon pepper
⅛ tsp. salt
½ tsp. dried parsley flakes, crushed
⅓ cup dry bread crumbs
1 Tbsp. margarine, melted

Preheat oven to 500°F. Cut fillets into small portions. Combine orange juice concentrate with lemon pepper, salt, and parsley. Dip fish into orange juice mixture, then roll into bread crumbs. Drizzle margarine over fillets. Bake for 10 to 15 minutes or until fish flakes easily.

Per serving
381 calories
146 mg cholesterol
421 mg sodium
1.5 gm saturated fat
9.1 gm fat

Exchanges per serving
½ bread
1½ fat
1 fruit
4 meat

On the side Mix steamed broccoli and carrots for a colorful side dish to this healthy dish. Serve the meal with a glass of non-fat milk and this dinner is nutritionally complete.

Nonstick cooking spray
4 walleye fillets

2 Tbsp. sugar
2 Tbsp. lemon juice
1 tsp. Worcestershire sauce
½ tsp. paprika
½ tsp. lemon pepper

Spray pan with nonstick spray. Mix sugar, lemon juice, Worcestershire sauce, paprika, and lemon pepper; set aside. Rinse fillets and pat dry. Place fillets on pan. Brush fillets with sauce. Broil, turning and basting, until fillets are flaky.

Per serving
103 calories
73 mg. cholesterol
43 mg sodium
0.2 gm saturated fat
1.0 gm fat

Exchanges per serving
2 meat

On the side Serve this fish dish with a side of white rice, some steamed carrots, a glass of milk, and fresh pears for dessert and you have a nutritionally complete meal.

Kettle of Fish

2 Tbsp. margarine, melted
3 large potatoes, thinly sliced
½ tsp. ginger
1 small zucchini, thinly sliced
2 cups tomato, peeled, seeded and sliced
½ cup green onions, sliced
1½ lb. haddock
¼ tsp. thyme
½ tsp. oregano
⅛ tsp. pepper
1 tsp. dried parsley flakes

Preheat oven to 350°F. Put melted margarine in oblong baking dish. Arrange sliced potatoes on bottom and sprinkle with ¼ of ginger. Cover and bake for 15 minutes. Place other vegetables on top of potatoes and layer the fish fillets on top. Sprinkle with seasonings and remaining ginger. Return to oven and bake for 20 minutes or until fish flakes easily.

Per serving
246 calories
33 mg cholesterol
47.6 mg sodium
0.75 gm saturated fat
6 gm fat

Exchanges per serving
½ bread
2 meat
1 vegetable

On the side This tasty fish stew is a complete meal in itself and needs only a glass of milk and an apple to make it nutritionally balanced.

Lamb

2 Tbsp. vegetable oil
6 lamp chops
2 cups tomatoes, chopped
1 Tbsp. red wine vinegar
1 tsp. dried basil
1 tsp. ginger
⅛ cup dry vermouth
⅛ tsp. pepper

Preheat oven to 375°F. In a large skillet, heat oil; brown chops on both sides. Remove and place in 9 x 13-inch baking pan. Combine remaining ingredients in the same skillet. Stir and cook for 3 minutes. Pour over chops and bake for 35 minutes. Baste meat with sauce occasionally.

Per serving
200 calories
51 mg cholesterol
179 mg sodium
3.3 gm saturated fat
12.1 gm fat

Exchanges per serving
1 fat
2 meat
1 vegetable

On the side Fresh cooked beets work well with this version of baked lamb chops. A dessert of apples and raisins in yogurt completes the meal.

Curried Lamb

Serves 4 **230**

2 Tbsp. margarine
¼ cup chopped onions
2½ tsp. curry powder
2 lb. lamb, cubed
1½ Tbsp. cornstarch
¾ cup raisins
1¾ cup low-fat yogurt
2 cups cooked rice

In skillet, melt margarine. Add onions and curry powder; sauté. Combine all ingredients except yogurt and rice; simmer until thick and smooth. Remove from heat and stir in yogurt. Serve over rice.

Per serving
375 calories
110 mg cholesterol
514 mg sodium
5.7 gm saturated fat
12.3 gm fat

Exchanges per serving
1 bread
1½ fat
2 meat
½ milk

On the side Minted carrots look great on the plate and add just the right flavor to enhance this spicy dish. Fresh pear slices for dessert and you've got a meal that's delicious and nutritious.

Serves 4

2 lbs. lamb steaks
3 tsp. Dijon-style mustard
3 tsp. honey
3 tsp. teriyaki sauce
1 Tbsp. minced garlic
2 Tbsp. low-calorie apricot spread

In bowl, combine all ingredients except lamb; mix well. On broiler pan, place lamb steaks and brush with mustard mixture. Broil 5 to 7 minutes; turn steaks over and baste. Broil until done to taste.

Per serving
197 calories
86 mg cholesterol
220 mg sodium
8.3 gm saturated fat
11.1 gm fat

Exchanges per serving
3 meat

On the side New potatoes with rosemary, green beans and garlic, and apple chunks and raisins with yogurt, topped with cinnamon, make this meal complete nutritionally.

Grilled Lamb Steaks

¼ cup balsamic vinegar
1 Tbsp. minced garlic
1 tsp. rosemary
¼ tsp. black pepper
4 6-oz. lamb steaks, trimmed of fat
Nonstick cooking spray

In a small bowl, combine vinegar, garlic, rosemary, and pepper. Place steaks on a platter. Rub vinegar mixture on both sides of steaks. Marinate for 2 hours. Lightly grease grill rack with cooking spray. Remove steaks from marinade and discard marinade. Grill steaks the way you like it, rare, medium, or well done.

Per serving
234 calories
111 mg cholesterol
81 mg sodium
4.7 gm saturated fat
12.4 gm fat

Exchanges per serving
4 meat

On the side Broccoli with garlic, 8 ounces nonfat milk, and a cup of mixed melon balls garnished with fresh mint complete this meal nutritionally.

1 lb. ground lamb
⅔ cup grated carrots
1 egg
1 cup finely chopped onions
⅓ cup Parmesan cheese
⅛ tsp. salt
⅛ tsp. pepper
1½ tsp. garlic
½ cup vegetable oil
2 Tbsp. lemon juice

In bowl, combine lamb, carrots, egg, onions, cheese, salt, pepper, and ½ tsp. garlic; blend well. Scoop out rounded tablespoons of the meat mixture and make balls. Spear lamb balls in the center with wooden kabob sticks—3 on a stick. Place in a shallow dish. Combine 1 tsp. garlic, oil, and lemon juice; mix. Pour over kabobs. Broil, turning kabobs and brushing with marinade. Broil to your desired taste.

Per serving
370 calories
132 mg cholesterol
174 mg sodium
9.58 gm saturated fat
20.0 gm fat

Exchanges per serving
1 fat
3 meat
1 vegetable

On the side Saffron rice, broccoli with garlic, and a dessert mousse of yogurt with pears and honeydew melon, whipped in the blender with ½ tsp. vanilla and fresh mint leaves make this meal complete nutritionally.

Lamb with Eggplant

1½ lb. ground lamb
1 cup chopped onions
1 small eggplant, sliced
1 cup tomatoes, chopped
1 tsp. garlic
1 8-oz. can low-sodium tomato sauce
⅛ tsp. pepper

In skillet, heat margarine and add lamb; cook until pink color disappears. Add remaining ingredients. Cover and cook over medium heat, stirring occasionally, for 20 minutes or until eggplant is done.

Per serving
319 calories
83 mg cholesterol
67 mg sodium
11.5 gm saturated fat
26.5 gm fat

Exchanges per serving
3 meat
1 vegetable

On the side Parsley new potatoes go well with this hearty lamb dish. For dessert make a plate of fresh fruits, sliced, and sprinkle them with poppy seeds. Offer a yogurt dip, and the meal is complete nutritionally.

4 lamb chops, 1-inch thick
1 Tbsp. sugar
1 tsp. cornstarch
⅔ cup unsweetened pineapple juice
¼ cup chopped red pepper
2 tsp. soy sauce
½ tsp. ground ginger
⅛ tsp. ground cloves

Preheat broiler. Trim fat from lamb chops. Place chops on broiling pan and broil until desired doneness. While chops are broiling, stir together sugar and corn-starch in a saucepan. Stir in pineapple juice, red pep-per, soy sauce, ginger, and cloves. Cook and stir until thickened and bubbly. Serve sauce over chops.

Per serving
267 calories
75 mg cholesterol
468 mg sodium
4.75 gm saturated fat
13.5 gm fat

Exchanges per serving
½ fruit
3 meat

On the side A serving of white rice, snow pea pods, lightly sautéed so they are still crunchy, and a strawberry milk shake (made with a cup of skim milk and ½ cup frozen strawberries) blended until frothy) complete this meal nutritionally.

Zucchini and Lamb Casserole

Serves 8 **236**

¼ cup low-sodium tomato paste
3 cups water
1 cup uncooked rice
1 tsp. cinnamon
6 small zucchinis, cut into slices
1 lb. ground lamb
⅛ tsp. pepper
1 tsp. dried parsley flakes

Preheat oven to 350°F. In skillet, brown lamb; drain. Lay zucchini on the bottom of a casserole dish and put lamb on top of zucchini. Mix together tomato paste, water, rice, cinnamon, parsley, and pepper. Pour over lamb and zucchini. Bake for 30 minutes.

Per serving
160 calories
41.9 mg cholesterol
33.9 mg sodium
5.8 gm saturated fat
13.3 gm fat

Exchanges per serving
½ bread
2 meat
1 vegetable

On the side Serve this casserole with ½ slices of a hearty whole-grain bread, a glass of milk, and an apple poached in honey for a nutritionally complete meal.

Pork
& Ham

1 egg white
⅓ cup quick cooking oats
¼ cup raisins
3 tsp. minced onion
2 tsp. prepared mustard
⅛ tsp. pepper
⅛ tsp. salt
1 cup applesauce
¼ tsp. cinnamon
1 lb. lean ground pork

Preheat oven to 350°F. In mixing bowl, beat egg white. Stir in oats, raisins, onion, mustard, pepper, salt, and ¼ cup applesauce. Add the pork and mix well. Shape into a loaf, then place in a baking pan. Bake for 55 to 60 minutes. In a saucepan, combine remaining applesauce and cinnamon. Cook until heated. To serve, slice loaf and serve with heated applesauce.

Per serving
323 calories
149 mg cholesterol
173 mg sodium
3.5 gm saturated fat
10.0 gm fat

Exchanges per serving
½ bread
½ fruit
3 meat

On the side Baby carrots, sautéed with margarine and gingerroot, go well with this novel variety of meat loaf. Add a glass of milk and this meal is nutritionally balanced.

Creole Pork Chops

2 lean pork chops, 1-inch thick
1 Tbsp. vegetable oil
⅔ cup chopped onions
⅔ cup chopped green pepper
¼ tsp. minced garlic
1 Tbsp. margarine
¾ cup chopped tomatoes
2 Tbsp. sweet vermouth
¾ tsp. oregano
⅛ tsp. basil

In a skillet, heat oil and brown pork chops; remove chops from pan. In same skillet, melt margarine; add onions, green peppers, and garlic; sauté until tender. Add remaining ingredients to skillet; simmer for 15 minutes, stirring frequently. Add pork chops and simmer for 25 minutes.

Per serving
300 calories
50 mg cholesterol
120 mg sodium
5.0 gm saturated fat
20.0 gm fat

Exchanges per serving
1½ fat
3 meat
1 vegetable

On the side Serve this colorful dish with white rice, green beans, steamed just until tender, and a side of fresh apple sauce just whipped up in the blender. Add a glass of milk and the meal is nutritionally complete.

6 pork chops, 1-inch thick
3 Tbsp. Dijon-style mustard
¾ cup plain bread crumbs
1½ tsp. curry powder
2 Tbsp. margarine, melted
1 Tbsp. dried, minced onion

Preheat oven to 400°F. Brush chops with mustard. In a dish, combine bread crumbs, curry powder, margarine and onions. Coat pork chops with crumb mixture. Put chops in a baking pan. Bake for 35 minutes.

Per serving
315 calories
70 mg cholesterol
177 mg sodium
9.6 gm saturated fat
23.5 gm fat

Exchanges per serving
½ bread
1 fat
3 meat

On the side Saffron rice, stir-fried cabbage bites, a dessert of baked apples with cinnamon, and a glass of milk make this meal nutritionally complete.

Fruited Pork Chops

8 lean pork chops
½ cup unsweetened apple juice
1 cup raisins
8 drops Tabasco sauce
¼ cup brown sugar
½ tsp. cinnamon
⅛ tsp. clove
⅛ tsp. nutmeg
⅔ cup water
4 large apples, each cut into 8 wedges

Preheat oven to 350°F. Brown pork chops in skillet on both sides. Arrange chops in shallow baking dish and pour in apple juice, Tabasco sauce, and raisins. Bake for 45 minutes. In a bowl, mix brown sugar, cinnamon, clove, and nutmeg. Add apples and coat apples with mixture. Turn chops in baking dish, arrange apples around the chops and sprinkle sugar mixture over apples and chops. Pour water over entire contents. Bake for 15 minutes.

Per serving
360 calories
63 mg cholesterol
228 mg sodium
3.48 gm saturated fat
10.1 gm fat

Exchanges per serving
2 fruit
2 meat

On the side A serving of brown rice or a slice of your favorite dark bread goes well with this spicy-fruity dish. Add a cabbage salad or a serving of green beans and a glass of milk and the meal is complete nutritionally.

2 pork loin chops
½ cup sliced carrots
½ cup unsweetened apple cider
¼ cup celery, chopped
⅓ cup chopped onion
¾ cup diced mango
¾ cup diced apple
¼ cup raisins
½ tsp. cinnamon

Preheat oven to 350°F. Place pork chops on broiling
pan and broil just until pork chops are lightly
browned and set aside. In an 8 x 8-inch baking dish,
combine all remaining ingredients; top with pork
chops. Cover and bake for 35 minutes.

Per serving
370 calories
70 mg cholesterol
250 mg sodium
6.0 gm saturated fat
15.0 gm fat

Exchanges per serving
2 fruit
3 meat
1 vegetable

On the side Serve this with white rice and a glass of milk and the
meal is complete nutritionally.

2 1-lb. cans black-eyed peas, rinsed and drained
1½ tsp. dried sage
1 8-oz. can low-sodium tomato sauce
1 tsp. garlic powder
1 cup carrots, grated
1 cup lean ham, diced
1½ Tbsp. vegetable oil
⅛ tsp. pepper

Preheat oven to 350°F. Mix all ingredients together in a mixing bowl. Put in a 9 x 13-inch pan. Cover and bake for 30 minutes.

Per serving
338 calories
55 mg cholesterol
681 mg sodium
6.0 gm saturated fat
20.2 gm fat

Exchanges per serving
2 bread
1 fat
1 meat
1 vegetable

On the side Here's a nutritious one-dish meal that needs only an apple-raisin salad and a glass of milk to be complete.

2 3-oz. slices boned, cooked ham
1 cup chunk pineapple in unsweetened juice
4 oz. peeled, cooked sweet potatoes, mashed
1 Tbsp. brown sugar
¼ tsp. ground cinnamon
1 Tbsp. margarine

Preheat oven to 350°F. In a baking dish, place ham and top with pineapple. Spread mashed sweet potatoes over pineapple, sprinkle with brown sugar and cinnamon and dot each with ½ tablespoon margarine. Bake for 20 minutes.

Per serving
177 calories
16 mg cholesterol
612 mg sodium
1.6 gm saturated fat
8.1 gm fat

Exchanges per serving
½ fruit
3 meat
1 fat

On the side Serve this with a slice of brown bread, a serving of green beans, lightly steamed, and a glass of milk for a nutritionally complete meal.

4 pork loin chops, ¾-inch thick
¾ tsp. orange peel
⅓ cup orange juice
⅓ cup pineapple juice
3 Tbsp. soy sauce
1 Tbsp. honey
⅛ tsp. pepper
½ tsp. minced garlic
1 Tbsp. cornstarch

Trim fat from chops. In shallow baking dish, combine orange peel, orange juice, pineapple juice, soy sauce, honey, pepper, and garlic. Add meat and turn to coat. Marinate for 2 to 3 hours. Place chops on broiler pan. Broil chops until desired doneness. Transfer marinade to a sauce pan. Stir in cornstarch and cook until thickened and bubbly; pass with chops.

Per serving
285 calories
70 mg cholesterol
669 mg sodium
8.9 gm saturated fat
12.0 gm fat

Exchanges per serving
1 fruit
3 meat

On the side White rice, zucchini squash, julienned and stir-fried, and a strawberry yogurt dessert makes this meal nutritionally complete.

4 pork tenderloin chops, ½-inch thick
1 8-oz. can cream of mushroom soup
¼ cup skim milk

In skillet, brown chops on both sides. Combine soup and milk. Pour over chops. Cover, cook for 20 to 25 minutes or until chops are tender.

Per serving
315 calories
79 mg cholesterol
323 mg sodium
2.0 gm saturated fat
6.3 gm fat

Exchanges per serving
1 fat
3 meat

On the side Boiled potatoes, cooked baby carrots, a glass of milk, and apples poached in honey for dessert make this meal nutritionally complete.

Mustard Pork Chops

2 Tbsp. Dijon-style mustard
3 tsp. lime juice
1 tsp. cumin
⅛ tsp. black pepper
1 lb. thin pork chops

Whisk mustard, lime juice, cumin, and pepper.
Arrange chops on broiling pan; broil on one side for 5
to 6 minutes with half mustard mixture spread on
chops. Turn and spread remaining mixture and broil
for 5 to 6 minutes more.

Per serving
301 calories
100 mg cholesterol
72 mg sodium
6.25 gm saturated fat
18.0 gm fat

Exchanges per serving
4 meat

On the side Green noodles, baby carrots, apple sauce from the
blender, and a glass of milk complete this meal nutritionally.

1 egg white
⅓ cup chopped onions
¾ tsp. ground oregano
⅛ tsp. salt
⅛ tsp. pepper
1 lb. lean ground pork
½ cup pizza sauce
½ cup part-skim shredded mozzarella cheese
2 cups shredded lettuce

Preheat broiler. In medium-sized mixing bowl, beat egg white. Stir in onion, oregano, salt, and pepper. Add pork and mix well. Shape meat mixture into four patties. Place patties on broiling pan and broil for about 12 to 15 minutes, turning once. Pour pizza sauce over patties and broil for a few minutes more. Sprinkle with cheese and broil until cheese melts. Divide lettuce among four serving plates. To serve, place meat patties on top of lettuce.

Per serving
320 calories
94 mg cholesterol
399 mg sodium
7.87 gm saturated fat
20.5 gm fat

Exchanges per serving
3 meat

On the side Serve these tasty patties on a plate or on a whole-wheat bun, add a tossed salad, and whip up a peachy milk shake in the blender. You've got a meal that's delicious and nutritionally complete.

Pork Chops with Dill

8 loin pork chops, ⅝-inch thick
½ tsp. ground pepper
2 tsp. crushed dill seed
2 Tbsp. olive oil
1 tsp. minced onion

Rub pork chops well with pepper, dill seed, olive oil, and onions. Broil for 10 minutes or until cooked through.

Per serving
315 calories
105 mg cholesterol
183 mg sodium
3.5 gm saturated fat
12.0 gm fat

Exchanges per serving
3 meat

On the side White rice, a salad of fresh cucumbers and onions, and a pear, poached in almond extract complete this meal nutritionally.

¾ lb. lean boneless pork, 1-inch thick
½ cup orange juice
1 tsp. finely grated orange peel
¼ cup soy sauce
1 Tbsp. brown sugar
⅛ tsp. ground ginger
1 10 oz. package frozen asparagus
2 carrots, cut into sticks

Cut pork on the bias into 3-inch strips. Combine orange juice, orange peel, soy sauce, brown sugar, and ginger. Place meat in a bowl and pour marinade over meat and marinate for several hours. Drain meat and reserve marinade. Cook vegetables in a small amount of water until crisp-tender. For each kabob, wrap meat strips around 1 or 2 asparagus spears and 1 carrot. Repeat with remaining meat and vegetables. Thread kabobs on skewers. Brush with reserve marinade. Broil until pork is done.

Per serving
294 calories
75 mg cholesterol
898 mg sodium
4.75 gm saturated fat
12.1 gm fat

Exchanges per serving
½ fruit
3 meat
1 vegetable

On the side Try our yams as a delightful accompaniment to this meal. A serving of cabbage, apple, raisin salad with yogurt dressing makes the meal complete nutritionally.

Pork Zucchini

8 oz. pork cubed steak
1½ cups sliced zucchini
⅔ cup chopped onions
½ cup tomato sauce
¼ cup chopped tomato
¼ tsp. thyme
⅛ tsp. salt
⅛ tsp. pepper
⅔ cup shredded mozzarella cheese, part-skim
2 pita bread rounds, halved

Cut pork into bite-size pieces. In a nonstick skillet, cook meat until no pink remains. Drain off fat. Add zucchini, onion, tomato sauce, tomatoes, thyme, salt, and pepper. Cook over medium heat until vegetables are crisp-tender, stirring occasionally. Divide meat-vegetable mixture among pita halves. Top each pita half with cheese.

Per serving
292 calories
68 mg cholesterol
342 mg sodium
6.25 gm saturated fat
14.5 gm fat

Exchanges per serving
1 bread
2 meat
1 vegetable

On the side Serve some fresh pineapple slices for dessert and add a glass of milk and the meal conforms to today's standard for total nutritional balance.

251 Ribs with Apple Butter

3 lbs. meaty pork spareribs
¾ cup apple butter
½ Tbsp. vinegar
¾ tsp. minced onion
½ tsp. garlic powder
1 Tbsp. water

Preheat oven to 450°F. Place ribs, meaty side down, in a shallow roasting pan. Roast for 30 minutes. Remove meat from oven; drain. Turn ribs and reduce oven to 350°F. Roast for another 30 minutes. Mix apple butter, vinegar, onion, garlic, and water. Pour mixture over ribs and roast for 30 minutes more.

Per serving
405 calories
143 mg cholesterol
201 mg sodium
9.6 gm saturated fat
20.5 gm fat

Exchanges per serving
2 fat
4 meat

On the side Twice-baked yams, cabbage salad, and dessert of baked apple slices with cinnamon round out this meal. Add a glass of milk for total nutritional balance.

Poultry

1 large chicken breast, skinned, halved
4 tsp. margarine
½ cup low-calorie apricot preserves
2 Tbsp. lemon juice
½ tsp. lemon rind
½ tsp. lemon pepper

Preheat oven to 350°F. Arrange chicken in baking pan and dot with margarine. In a saucepan, combine apricot preserves, lemon juice, lemon rind and lemon pepper; cook over low heat until preserves melt and mixture is blended. Pour over chicken and bake, uncovered, for 35 to 40 minutes. Baste occasionally.

Per serving
371 calories
43 mg cholesterol
133 mg sodium
1.9 mg sodium
1.9 gm saturated fat
9.8 gm fat

Exchanges per serving
1 fat
1 fruit
3 meat

On the side White rice, steamed green beans, and a glass of milk make this meal nutritionally complete and delicious.

Baked Chicken

2 boneless, skinless chicken breasts, halved
½ cup skim milk
⅓ cup herb-seasoned bread crumbs
⅛ tsp. paprika

Preheat oven to 400°F. Dip chicken in skim
milk and roll in bread crumbs. Place chicken
in baking pan. Sprinkle chicken with paprika.
Bake 30 to 35 minutes.

Per serving
162 calories
70 mg cholesterol
138 mg sodium
0.5 gm saturated fat
3.0 gm fat

Exchanges per serving
2 meat

On the side New potatoes with rosemary, a tossed salad, and a
peachy milk shake make this meal nutritionally complete.

3 lb. fryer chicken, cut into pieces
⅛ tsp. garlic powder
1 cup low-calorie apricot preserves
½ cup chopped onions
3 Tbsp. soy sauce
½ cup bottled barbecue sauce

Preheat oven to 375°F. Arrange chicken in a baking dish. Sprinkle with garlic powder. Bake for 20 minutes. In a bowl, combine remaining ingredients. Spoon over chicken and bake for 20 minutes more or until chicken is done.

Per serving
305 calories
153 mg cholesterol
590 mg sodium
3.55 gm saturated fat
10 gm fat

Exchanges per serving
1 fruit
3 meat

On the side White rice, sautéed vegetables, and a glass of milk complete this meal nutritionally.

2 boneless, skinned chicken breasts, halved
¼ cup low-sodium soy sauce
½ tsp. garlic powder
1 tsp. dried basil

Baste chicken with soy sauce. Sprinkle chicken with garlic powder and basil. Broil chicken. Baste with soy sauce as chicken broils.

Per serving
173 calories
73 mg cholesterol
825 mg sodium
1.7 gm saturated fat
5.3 gm fat

Exchanges per serving
1½ meat
1 bread

On the side Fresh corn on the cob, a plate of crisp vegetables with dilled yogurt dip, and watermelon slices (a 4 x 8-inch wedge equals one fruit and 110 calories) make this meal balanced nutritionally.

Nonstick cooking spray
2 whole chicken breasts, boneless, skinned, halved
½ cup margarine, melted
¼ cup lemon juice
1 Tbsp. dried parsley flakes
¼ tsp. salt
⅛ tsp. black pepper

Spray broiler pan with nonstick spray. Place chicken on broiler pan. Mix all ingredients together. Baste chicken with sauce. Broil, turning and basting until chicken is done.

Per serving
268 calories
74 mg cholesterol
209 mg sodium
2.3 gm saturated fat
12 gm fat

Exchanges per serving
½ bread
3 meat

On the side A serving of white rice, broccoli, steamed just until tender and seasoned with a little lemon juice, a glass of milk and fresh pineapple slices for dessert give this meal nutritional balance.

Broiled Tarragon Chicken

Serves 6 **257**

2 2½-lb chickens, cut into parts and skinned
1 cup chopped onions
¾ cup peanut oil
2 Tbsp. dried tarragon
½ tsp. hot pepper sauce

Combine all ingredients in large bowl. Put chicken in and marinate chicken in refrigerator for about 1 hour, turning the chicken from time to time. Place chicken on broiler pan. Broil; turn and baste with marinade. Broil until chicken is tender.

Per serving
250 calories
89 mg cholesterol
86 mg sodium
1 gm saturated fat
9 gm fat

Exchanges per serving
1 fat
3 meat

On the side A serving of white rice, baby carrots simmered with gingerroot, and a strawberry milk shake complete this meal nutritionally.

4 oz. curly noodles
1 10-oz. can cream of chicken soup
½ cup skim milk
⅔ cup low-fat cottage cheese
1 cup chopped, cooked, skinless chicken breast
⅔ cup part-skim shredded American cheese, divided
½ tsp. crushed tarragon

Preheat oven to 350°F. Cook noodles according to package directions; drain. In a bowl, combine soup and milk. Stir in cottage cheese, chicken, half of the cheese, and tarragon. Mix in the noodles. Pour mixture into a casserole dish. Cover and bake for 30 minutes. Sprinkle remaining cheese on top. Bake for 5 minutes more.

Per serving
296 calories
51 mg cholesterol
841 mg sodium
5 gm saturated fat
9 gm fat

Exchanges per serving
2 bread
1 fat
3 meat

On the side A mixed vegetable, like green beans and carrots, or broccoli and cauliflower goes well with this casserole. Add a glass of milk and some fresh fruit for dessert and the meal is complete nutritionally.

Chicken à la King

2 Tbsp. margarine
1½ cups sliced mushrooms
⅓ cup flour
⅛ tsp. salt
⅛ tsp. pepper
2 cups skim milk
¾ cup low-sodium chicken broth
2 cups cubed, cooked chicken
½ cup frozen peas, thawed
2 tsp. sherry
4 slices whole wheat bread, toasted

In a saucepan, melt margarine. Add mushrooms and cook until tender. Stir in flour, salt and pepper. Add milk and chicken broth. Cook and stir until thickened and bubbly. Stir in chicken, peas, and sherry. Heat through. Serve over toasted bread.

Per serving
375 calories
107 mg cholesterol
473 mg sodium
3.6 gm saturated fat
16 gm fat

Exchanges per serving
1½ bread
1 fat
2 meat
½ skim milk
½ vegetable

On the side This one-dish meal needs only a plate of fresh mixed fruits and a yogurt dip for dessert and it is nutritionally complete.

2 chicken breasts, skinless, boneless
1½ cups low-sodium chicken broth
1½ Tbsp. lime juice
½ tsp. crushed basil
½ tsp. crushed oregano
⅛ tsp. celery seed
½ tsp. lime rind, grated

Preheat oven to 325°F. Place chicken in shallow baking dish. Combine broth, lime juice, basil, oregano, celery seed and lime rind; pour over the chicken. Cover and bake for 45 to 50 minutes.

Per serving
230 calories
61 mg cholesterol
78 mg sodium
1.4 gm saturated fat
5.3 gm fat

Exchanges per serving
3 meat

On the side Baked potato sticks, fresh cooked spinach, and a peachy milk shake make this meal nutritionally complete.

1 5-lb. roasting chicken
⅛ tsp. salt
⅛ tsp. pepper
½ tsp. dried rosemary
¾ tsp. ground cumin
1 tsp. paprika
1 tsp. minced garlic
4 Tbsp. vegetable oil

Preheat oven to 325°F. Combine in a bowl, all ingredients, except chicken. Rub entire surface of the chicken with seasoned oil mixture. Put chicken in a cooking bag and place bag in roasting pan. Bake for 2½ to 3 hours.

Per serving
322 calories
66 mg cholesterol
153 mg sodium
5.6 gm saturated fat
23.5 gm fat

Exchanges per serving
1 fat
3½ meat

On the side A serving of new potatoes with parsley, broccoli with garlic, a glass of milk, and a poached pear give this meal complete nutritional balance.

2 whole chicken breasts, boneless, skinless
3 Tbsp. soy sauce
1 Tbsp. vegetable oil
1 20 oz. package frozen broccoli, thawed
¾ cup low sodium chicken broth
½ cup sliced, fresh mushrooms
½ cup sliced bamboo shoots
2 tsp. lemon juice
¾ Tbsp. cornstarch

Cut chicken into slices. In bowl, combine chicken, soy sauce, and oil; set aside. In skillet, place broccoli and ½ cup broth and stir-fry on medium heat until broccoli is crisp-tender. Increase heat to high; add chicken mixture. Stir-fry for 3 minutes. Add mushrooms and bamboo shoots; stir-fry for 1 minute. Decrease heat. Combine lemon juice, cornstarch, and remaining ½ cup broth. Stir into chicken mixture; heat until thickened.

Per serving
220 calories
22.9 mg cholesterol
496 mg sodium
0.4 gm saturated fat
3.4 gm fat

Exchanges per serving
½ bread
2 meat
1 vegetable

On the side A serving of white rice, a glass of milk, and a dessert of melon balls and berries balance this meal nutritionally.

Chicken Cacciatore

1 Tbsp. vegetable oil
1 Tbsp. minced garlic
3 chicken breasts, skinned and cut in halves
¾ cup chopped onion
¾ cup chopped green pepper
1 cup fresh tomatoes, peeled and chopped
¼ tsp. basil
⅛ tsp. pepper
¼ tsp. rosemary
¼ cup dry white wine

Heat oil and garlic in skillet. Add chicken and brown. Remove chicken. Add onions and green pepper; cook until tender. Pour off fat. Return chicken to skillet. Add remaining ingredients. Cover and simmer until chicken is tender.

Per serving
175 calories
36 mg cholesterol
41.4 mg sodium
0.6 gm saturated fat
3.9 gm fat

Exchanges per serving
2 meat
1 vegetable

On the side Green noodles go very well with this Italian-style chicken dish. A dessert of watermelon and honeydew melon balls and a glass of milk make the meal complete nutritionally.

1 Tbsp. dried dillweed
1 Tbsp. lemon pepper
1 cup Wheaties, crushed
2 chicken breasts, boneless, skinless, cut in half
1 egg
1½ Tbsp. margarine, melted

Heat oven to 375°F. In shallow dish, combine dillweed, lemon pepper, and Wheaties. In a bowl, beat egg until mixed. Dip chicken into egg and then into dry ingredients. Place in baking dish. Drizzle margarine over chicken. Bake 35 to 40 minutes.

Per serving
248 calories
136 mg cholesterol
147 mg sodium
6.11 gm saturated fat
11.25 gm fat

Exchanges per serving
½ bread
1 fat
2½ meat

On the side Add a small dinner roll, cauliflower, steamed just until tender, a glass of milk and a fresh peach for dessert and this meal is complete nutritionally.

1 lb. boneless, skinned chicken breasts
3 cups fresh broccoli spears
3 Tbsp. margarine
½ cup chopped onion
¼ cup flour
1½ cups skim milk
⅛ tsp. black pepper

Preheat oven to 400°F. In nonstick skillet, brown chicken breasts. Steam broccoli spears. In saucepan, melt margarine. Add onions and cook. Stir in flour. Gradually add milk and pepper. Cook until thickened and smooth. In an 8-inch baking dish, place chicken in dish. Sprinkle broccoli over chicken. Pour mixture over chicken and broccoli. Bake 20 minutes until bubbly.

Per serving
335 calories
83 mg cholesterol
230 mg sodium
2.9 gm saturated fat
13.2 gm fat

Exchanges per serving
1 fat
3 meat
½ skim milk
1 vegetable

On the side Roasted potatoes with rosemary add the bread course, and a fruit plate with yogurt dip add a fruit and milk to make this meal nutritionally complete.

2 Tbsp. vegetable oil
1 tsp. minced garlic
1 16-oz. can stewed tomatoes without salt
4 tsp. chili powder
⅛ tsp. ground pepper
2 cups cooked, chopped chicken
½ cup plain low-fat yogurt
2 Tbsp. green chilies
1 Tbsp. chopped green onion
1 Tbsp. minced onion
4 corn tortillas
1 cup part-skim mozzarella cheese

Heat 1 tablespoon oil in saucepan. Add garlic and cook for about 1 minute. Add tomatoes, 3 teaspoons chili powder and pepper. Simmer for about 30 minutes, stirring occasionally. In bowl, combine cooked chicken, yogurt, green chilies, green onions, minced onion, and 1 teaspoon chili powder. Mix well. In skillet, heat remaining oil. Add tortillas and cook each side until soft. Preheat oven to 350°F. Spoon ¼ cup sauce in 8-inch square baking dish. Spread an equal amount of chicken mixture in center of each tortilla. Fold sides over filling. Place tortillas, seam side down in baking dish. Pour remaining sauce over tortillas. Sprinkle with cheese. Bake 30 minutes.

Per serving
326 calories
50 mg cholesterol
297 mg sodium
4.05 gm saturated fat
16 gm fat

Exchanges per serving
1 bread
1 fat
2 meat
1 vegetable

On the side Rice goes well with this meal. Add a glass of milk and a baked apple and the meal is nutritionally balanced.

¾ cup fresh chopped pineapple
½ cup sliced green onions
⅛ cup chopped celery
1 Tbsp. grated fresh ginger
2 chicken breasts
1 Tbsp. vegetable oil
3 Tbsp. soy sauce

Preheat oven to 350°F. Cover the bottom of a baking dish with pineapple, green onions, celery and ginger. Lay chicken on top. In a small bowl, mix oil and soy sauce. Pour over chicken. Cover and bake for 35 to 40 minutes.

Per serving
277 calories
85 mg cholesterol
85 mg sodium
2.1 gm saturated fat
11.5 gm fat

Exchanges per serving
1 fat
½ fruit
3 meat

On the side White rice, baby carrots, simmered with gingerroot, and a dessert of fresh fruit slices with yogurt dip make this meal nutritionally complete.

1 Tbsp. margarine
⅓ cup honey
1 Tbsp. prepared mustard
⅛ tsp. salt
¼ tsp. curry powder
2 Tbsp. soy sauce
⅛ tsp. pepper
2 large chicken breasts, skinned and cut in half

Preheat oven to 350°F. Melt margarine and mix in remaining ingredients, except chicken. Place chicken in a casserole dish and pour sauce over chicken. Bake 30 to 35 minutes, basting occasionally.

Per serving
211 calories
43 mg cholesterol
193 gm sodium
1.2 gm saturated fat
5.3 gm fat

Exchanges per serving
1 fat
2 meat

On the side Saffron rice, snow pea pods, sautéed just until crisp-tender, a glass of milk and a fresh fruit for dessert make this meal complete nutritionally.

Chicken in Cream Sauce

2 Tbsp. canola oil
1 lb. boneless, skinless chicken breasts
¼ cup chopped onion
1 tsp. minced garlic
1 cup chopped carrots, zucchini, basil, thyme
1 cup low-sodium chicken broth
⅛ tsp. salt
⅛ tsp. ground pepper
1 tomato, peeled and chopped
⅛ cup low-fat yogurt
⅛ cup skim milk
2 tsp. Dijon-style mustard
2 cups cooked rice

In skillet, heat 1 tablespoon oil. Add chicken and
brown on each side; remove to platter. Add remaining
oil to skillet and sauté onion and garlic. Add carrots,
zucchini, basil and thyme; sauté, stirring frequently.
Return chicken to skillet. Add chicken broth, salt and
pepper. Simmer for 10 minutes, turning chicken once.
Remove chicken and vegetables to platter and keep
warm. In skillet, add tomatoes, yogurt, milk and mustard. Increase heat and cook, stirring vegetables until
sauce in slightly thickened. Spoon over chicken and
vegetables. Serve with rice.

Per serving
385 calories
98 mg cholesterol
472 mg sodium
1.9 gm saturated fat
11 gm fat

Exchanges per serving
1 bread
1 fat
3 meat
1 vegetable

On the side Add only a glass of milk and a piece of fruit to
complete this meal nutritionally.

4 boned, skinned chicken breast halves
⅓ cup low-fat yogurt
4 tsp. flour
⅛ cup water
1 tsp. curry powder
⅛ tsp. garlic powder
⅛ tsp. paprika
⅛ tsp. lemon pepper
2 10-oz. packages frozen broccoli spears
⅛ cup chopped peanuts

Preheat oven to 400°F. Place chicken in shallow baking dish. Cover with foil and bake for 20 to 25 minutes. While chicken is baking, combine yogurt and flour; set aside. In a pan, stir together water, curry powder, garlic powder, paprika and lemon pepper; bring to a boil. Reduce heat and add yogurt mixture. Cook until thickened. Cook broccoli according to package directions; drain. Pour sauce over chicken and top with peanuts; serve with broccoli.

Per serving
229 calories
76 mg cholesterol
116 mg sodium
1.75 gm saturated fat
7 gm fat

Exchanges per serving
1 fat
2½ meat
1 vegetable

On the side Serve this with brown rice, and offer a plate of fresh fruits with poppy seeds and yogurt dip for dessert and the meal is complete nutritionally.

Chicken in Mushroom Sauce

Serves 4 **271**

½ cup skim milk
½ cup cream of celery soup
½ cup cream of mushroom soup
1 cup sliced fresh mushrooms
2 whole chicken breasts, boneless, skinless

Heat oven to 375°F. Mix milk with soups until
smooth. Stir in mushrooms. Place chicken in baking
dish and pour mushroom mixture over chicken. Bake
35 to 40 minutes.

Per serving
213 calories
76 mg cholesterol
258 mg sodium
2.17 gm saturated fat
6.3 gm fat

Exchanges per serving
½ bread
2½ meat

On the side New potatoes, boiled, broccoli, cooked al dente, a
glass of milk and a fresh fruit for dessert complete this meal
nutritionally.

1 Tbsp. vegetable oil
1½ Tbsp. flour
12 oz. boneless, skinless chicken breasts
½ cup low-sodium chicken broth
¾ tsp. dry mustard
1 tsp. cornstarch
1 tsp. dried parsley flakes
1 Tbsp. sherry
⅓ cup low-fat ricotta cheese
⅓ cup low-fat plain yogurt

In skillet, heat oil. Flour chicken breasts and brown chicken on both sides. Remove and keep warm. Stir in chicken broth, mustard, cornstarch, parsley, and sherry until mixture thickens. Return chicken to pan. Mix ricotta cheese and yogurt until smooth. Stir in ricotta mixture; heat. Serve chicken with sauce.

Per serving
378 calories
88 mg cholesterol
109 mg sodium
5.3 gm saturated fat
12 gm fat

Exchanges per serving
1½ fat
4 meat

On the side A serving of white rice, fresh broccoli florets, steamed just until tender, and a peachy milk shake complete this meal nutritionally.

Nonstick cooking spray
8 oz. skinned, boned chicken breasts
⅛ tsp. salt
⅛ tsp. pepper
1 cup drained sauerkraut
⅓ cup shredded, part-skim provolone cheese
2 Tbsp. low-calorie Russian dressing
¼ cup part-skim Swiss cheese, shredded

Preheat oven to 350°F. Spray baking dish with non-stick spray. Set chicken in bottom of dish and sprinkle with salt and pepper. Spread sauerkraut over chicken and sprinkle with cheeses. Drizzle dressing over cheese. Cover and bake for 20 minutes.

Per serving
515 calories
200 mg cholesterol
2040 mg sodium
3 gm saturated fat
15 gm fat

Exchanges per serving
2 fat
4 meat
1 vegetable

On the side Serve this with a slice of your favorite brown bread, some beets, a glass of milk, and a baked apple for dessert to complete this meal nutritionally.

1 10-oz. package frozen brussel sprouts, thawed
2 whole chicken breasts, cut into strips
dash salt
dash pepper
1 Tbsp. vegetable oil
½ cup chopped onion
1½ tsp. lemon juice
¾ tsp. crushed basil
2 cups tomatoes, coarsely chopped

Put brussel sprouts in a colander and run hot water over them; drain and halve. Set aside. Remove skin from chicken; season with salt and pepper. In a skillet, heat oil and cook chicken strips and onion on medium-high heat until done. Stir in brussel sprouts, lemon juice, and basil. Reduce heat and cook for 10 minutes. Stir in tomatoes. Cook for 2 minutes more.

Per serving
164 calories
43 mg cholesterol
123 mg sodium
1.15 gm saturated fat
5.75 gm fat

Exchanges per serving
2 meat
1 vegetable

On the side Baked potato sticks are great with this chicken dish. Make yourself a milkshake using 8 ounces nonfat milk, ¼ cup fresh pineapple, and 6 ripe fresh strawberries. Garnish it with some fresh mint from the garden and your meal is nutritionally complete.

1½ lb. chicken breasts, boneless, skinned
⅔ cup oyster sauce
3 Tbsp. soy sauce
3 Tbsp. hoisin sauce*
¼ cup white wine
¼ cup water
⅛ tsp. pepper
¼ cup sliced green onions
1 Tbsp. vegetable oil

Cut chicken in large chunks. In a bowl, combine all ingredients except oil; mix well. Marinate chicken for 10 to 15 minutes. Remove chicken and place in a skillet with heated oil. Pour sauce over chicken and cook for 25 minutes or until chicken is done.

Available in the Oriental food section of most grocery stores.

Per serving
365 calories
145 mg cholesterol
286 mg sodium
2.6 gm saturated fat
8 gm fat

Exchanges per serving
1 fat
3 meat

On the side White rice, stir-fried snow pea pods, and a frozen, blended dessert of fresh pear slices, 2 teaspoons Creme de Menthe, and 8 ounces nonfat milk, served like ice cream, complete this meal deliciously and nutritiously.

1 whole chicken
1 can cream of celery soup
1 cup chicken broth
½ cup frozen peas
½ cup margarine
1 cup skim milk
¾ cup flour

Preheat oven to 400°F. Cook chicken in 2 quarts water. When done, remove chicken. De-bone chicken and put in 13 x 9 inch baking dish. Save 1 cup of broth. Combine cream of celery soup, broth and peas; heat over low until mixed. Pour over chicken. Melt margarine in sauce-pan. Add milk and mix in flour; mix well. Spoon over chicken mixture until well-coated. Bake for 40 to 45 minutes until golden brown.

Per serving
364 calories
84 mg cholesterol
331 mg sodium
4.46 gm saturated fat
18.75 gm fat

Exchanges per serving
1 bread
1 fat
2½ meat
½ skim milk

On the side Serve this tasty chicken pie with cooked carrots. Make a pretty fruit plate of mixed fruit slices and yogurt dip for dessert. The meal is complete nutritionally.

Chicken Pockets

Serves 4 **277**

Dressing:

½ cup plain, low-fat yogurt

1 tsp. finely chopped parsley

1 tsp. sugar

½ tsp. celery seed

2 Tbsp. skim milk

1 tsp. Dijon-style mustard

1 tsp. lemon juice

2 whole-wheat pocket pita breads

½ lb. cooked chicken, cubed

¾ cup alfalfa sprouts

¾ cup broccoli florets

¼ cup onion

In a bowl, combine dressing ingredients; blend well and refrigerate 1 hour. Spoon ⅛ cup yogurt mixture into each pocket bread half. Fill each half with ¼ of the chicken, sprouts, broccoli and onions.

Per serving
195 calories
25 mg cholesterol
207 mg sodium
2 gm saturated fat
6.5 gm fat

Exchanges per serving
½ bread
1 meat
1 vegetable
½ skim milk

On the side A glass of milk and honeydew melon slices for dessert give this meal nutritional balance.

1 cup low-sodium chicken broth
2 whole chicken breasts, boned, skinned, cubed
2 cups sliced zucchini
1 small eggplant, peeled and cubed
1 cup chopped onions
2 cups sliced mushrooms
2 tomatoes, cut into wedges
2 tsp. minced garlic
1 tsp. basil
1 tsp. oregano
1 Tbsp. soy sauce
¼ tsp. cayenne pepper

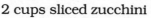
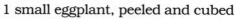

In large skillet, heat chicken broth and add the chicken. Sauté chicken on both sides. Add zucchini, eggplant, onions, and mushrooms and cook until tender; stir occasionally. Add tomatoes, garlic, basil, oregano, soy sauce, and cayenne. Simmer for 10 minutes.

Per serving
177 calories
48 mg cholesterol
146 mg sodium
0.6 gm saturated fat
2.0 gm fat

Exchanges per serving
2 meat
1 vegetable

On the side A serving of white rice, a glass of milk, and fresh fruit for dessert make this meal complete nutritionally.

1 cup low-sodium chicken broth
1 cup chopped onion
1 can sliced water chestnuts
¼ cup chopped red peppers
¾ tsp. sage
⅛ tsp. rosemary
1 10-oz. package frozen peas, thawed
1 12-oz. can low-sodium tomato purée
1 whole chicken breast, skinned, boned, cubed
4 cups cooked rice
6 egg whites, beaten stiff

Preheat oven to 350°F. In a saucepan, heat chicken broth. Add onion, water chestnuts, and red pepper; sauté until thoroughly cooked. Stir in the sage, rosemary and peas; simmer for 5 minutes. Add tomato purée and chicken. Put the cooked rice in a large bowl and mix in tomato-chicken sauce; fold in egg whites. Place in a baking dish, cover, and bake for 30 to 35 minutes.

Per serving
268 calories
43 mg cholesterol
468 mg sodium
0.14 gm saturated fat
2.6 gm fat

Exchanges per serving
1 bread
2 meat
1 vegetable

On the side You need only a milk and a fruit exchange to complete this meal nutritionally.

4 Tbsp. dry bread crumbs
2 Tbsp. grated Romano cheese
½ tsp. dried parsley flakes
½ tsp. dried basil
½ tsp. minced garlic
¼ cup skim milk
4 boned, skinned, chicken breast halves

Preheat oven to 425°F. In a dish, combine bread crumbs, Romano cheese, parsley, basil and minced garlic. Pour milk into another dish. Dip chicken in milk, then roll in the crumb mixture. Place chicken in a baking pan. Bake for 15 minutes or until chicken is tender.

Per serving
177 calories
82 mg cholesterol
163 mg sodium
1.25 gm saturated fat
6 gm fat

Exchanges per serving
3 meat

On the side This tasty chicken dish goes well with green noodles, cauliflower florets, steamed, and, for the fruit and milk choice, try blending fresh melon pieces into a glass of nonfat milk.

Chicken Salad

4 tsp. light mayonnaise
4 tsp. lemon juice
⅛ tsp. black pepper
⅛ tsp. thyme
⅛ tsp. sage
1 lb. boneless, skinless, cooked chicken, cubed
1 cup diced cucumber
¼ cup diced celery
¼ cup diced carrots
¼ cup chopped onion
1 tsp. dried parsley leaves

In a bowl, combine mayonnaise, lemon juice, pepper, thyme and sage; blend well. Add remaining ingredients and toss well.

Per serving
191 calories
74 mg cholesterol
27 mg sodium
1.61 gm saturated fat
5.85 gm fat

Exchanges per serving
1 fat
2 meat

On the side This salad tastes great with lettuce wedges, a slice of bread, a glass of milk, and a fresh orange for dessert.

½ cup low-sodium chicken broth
¼ cup light soy sauce
1 Tbsp. cornstarch
⅛ tsp. black pepper
1 lb. boneless, skinless chicken breasts
1 Tbsp. vegetable oil
2 cups sliced, fresh mushrooms
¼ cup chopped green onion
1 cup chopped green peppers
1 cup chopped carrots
1 cup chopped zucchini
1 tsp. minced garlic
¼ tsp. ginger

Cut chicken into chunks. In a bowl, combine chicken broth, soy sauce, cornstarch and ground pepper. Add chicken, mix well. Refrigerate for about 1 hour. In a large skillet, heat oil. Add mushrooms, green onion, green pepper, carrot, zucchini, garlic and ginger. Cook until crisp-tender; set aside. Add chicken to skillet with marinade. Cook, stirring occasionally until chicken is tender and sauce is thickened. Return vegetables to skillet. Cook until heated.

Per serving
160 calories
21 mg cholesterol
867 mg sodium
1.4 gm saturated fat
9.4 gm fat

Exchanges per serving
1 bread
2½ meat
1 vegetable

On the side White rice, a glass of milk and fresh pears complete this meal.

Chicken Tandoori

4 boneless, skinned chicken breasts, halved
1 cup low-fat, plain yogurt
1 tsp. ginger
¼ tsp. garlic powder
¼ tsp. ground cloves
¾ tsp. cinnamon
2 bay leaves
⅛ tsp. salt

Cut chicken into finger length strips. Mix together remaining ingredients and marinate for 3 hours. Bake in a casserole dish for 1 hour at 325°F.

Per serving
189 calories
73 mg cholesterol
67 mg sodium
1.3 gm saturated fat
8.1 gm fat

Exchanges per serving
2 meat
½ skim milk

On the side White rice with saffron, baby carrots, simmered with gingerroot, and a dessert of fresh fruits, sprinkled with poppy seeds and served with a yogurt dip, complete this tasty meal nutritionally.

2 2-lb. frying chickens
⅛ tsp. salt
⅛ tsp. pepper
⅔ cup orange juice
⅔ cup seedless raisins
⅛ cup chopped chutney
1 tsp. cinnamon
¼ tsp. curry powder
⅛ tsp. allspice

Preheat oven to 400°F. Place chicken in casserole dish and season with salt and pepper. Bake for 20 to 25 minutes. Mix remaining ingredients. Cover chicken with sauce; reduce heat to 250°F and bake for 50 minutes.

Per serving
360 calories
134 mg cholesterol
177 mg sodium
5.8 gm saturated fat
15.2 gm fat

Exchanges per serving
1 fruit
4 meat

On the side A serving of white rice, a side of baby carrots, and a glass of milk complete this meal nutritionally.

Chicken with Fresh Herbs

4 boned, skinned chicken breasts, halved
2 Tbsp. margarine, melted
½ Tbsp. basil
½ Tbsp. tarragon

Place chicken in a shallow baking pan. Mix margarine
and herbs together, pour over chicken and bake at
350°F for 45 minutes.

Per serving
190 calories
71 mg cholesterol
35 mg sodium
1.9 gm saturated fat
4.1 gm fat

Exchanges per serving
1 fat
2 meat

On the side We like this dish with green noodles, a melange of
mixed peppers as the vegetable, a glass of milk and fresh
peaches for dessert.

2 large boneless, skinned chicken breasts
⅛ tsp. salt
⅛ tsp. black pepper
3 Tbsp. margarine
3 cups low-sodium chicken broth
¼ cup flour
½ cup vermouth
⅛ tsp. cayenne pepper
1 cup seedless green grapes, halved

Cut chicken breast in half. Season with salt and pepper. Heat margarine in a skillet; sauté chicken until brown. Add one cup chicken broth and simmer for 20 minutes. Whisk together flour, vermouth, and remaining chicken broth. Add to cooked chicken and whisk until smooth. Sprinkle with cayenne pepper. Add grapes. Serve.

Per serving
276 calories
43 mg cholesterol
185 mg sodium
2.1 gm saturated fat
11.8 gm fat

Exchanges per serving
1 fat
½ fruit
3 meat

On the side White rice or green noodles go well with this entree. We like to serve baby carrots, simmered just until tender with some gingerroot, and offer a dessert of fruit slices, sprinkled with poppy seeds, with a yogurt dip. This complete the meal nutritionally, adds to eye appeal, and really pleases the palate.

9 oz. package frozen spinach
2 Tbsp. margarine
½ cup whole wheat bread crumbs
½ tsp. basil
⅛ tsp. black pepper
2 boneless, skinless chicken breasts, halved
½ cup part skim mozzarella cheese, shredded

Sauté spinach with 1 Tbsp. margarine. In a small bowl, combine bread crumbs, basil and pepper. Coat chicken with bread crumb mixture, pressing firmly. In skillet, heat remaining margarine. Brown chicken on both sides. Spoon spinach onto chicken and sprinkle cheese on top. Cover and cook until chicken is tender.

Per serving
276 calories
65 mg cholesterol
335 mg sodium
5.4 gm saturated fat
12.2 gm fat

Exchanges per serving
½ bread
1 fat
2 meat
1 vegetable

On the side You can choose to complete the bread exchange at this meal by adding a ½ slice of bread or a small dinner roll. A glass of milk and a fruit compote of melon balls and strawberries, sprinkled with crushed mint leaves, add the milk and fruit exchanges and complete the meal nutritionally.

1 cup low-fat plain yogurt
1 tsp. ground ginger
⅔ cup chopped onion
1 tsp. minced garlic
⅛ tsp. pepper
3 boneless, skinless, whole chicken breasts, split
¾ cup bread crumbs
¼ cup margarine, melted

Preheat oven to 350°F. In a dish, combine yogurt, ginger, onion, garlic and pepper. Add chicken and coat well. Dip chicken in crumbs to coat. Place chicken in baking dish. Drizzle with margarine. Bake for 20 to 25 minutes or until chicken is done.

Per serving
311 calories
71 mg cholesterol
205 mg sodium
2.5 gm saturated fat
9.3 gm fat

Exchanges per serving
½ bread
1 fat
3 meat

On the side We like to offer slices of pumpernickel or rye bread with this dish, cauliflower and broccoli florets mixed, and a strawberry milk shake to make the meal complete nutritionally.

Chinese Ginger Chicken

1 4-lb. skinned chicken, cut into 8 pieces
½ cup ginger brandy
¼ cup honey
½ cup soy sauce
½ cup low-sodium chicken broth
3 Tbsp. lemon juice
½ tsp. ground ginger
⅛ tsp. pepper

Combine all ingredients in large bowl. Refrigerate for several hours. Preheat oven to 350°F. Arrange chicken in shallow baking dish. Brush with brandy mixture. Bake for 40 minutes.

Per serving
258 calories
71 mg cholesterol
825 mg sodium
4.3 gm saturated fat
8.3 gm fat

Exchanges per serving
3 meat

On the side White rice, stir-fried snow pea pods, and a glass of milk work well with this flavorful oriental-style dish. A dessert of pears poached in almond extract completes the meal nutritionally.

2 Tbsp. margarine
2 Tbsp. flour
1½ cup low-sodium chicken broth
1 lb. skinned, boned, cooked chicken, cubed
2½ tsp. dillweed
⅛ tsp. pepper
⅓ cup plain low-fat yogurt

In saucepan, melt margarine. Add flour and stir constantly for 1 minute. Stir in broth and simmer for 5 minutes, stirring occasionally. Add chicken and dill. Simmer until chicken is hot. Season with pepper. Stir in yogurt and heat.

Per serving
218 calories
73 mg cholesterol
73 mg sodium
1.91 gm saturated fat
8.35 gm fat

Exchanges per serving
2 meat

On the side We like this with green noodles as the bread course. Fresh cucumber slices, a glass of milk, and a baked apple round out the meal nutritionally.

Crumb Chicken

2 4-oz. boneless, skinned chicken breasts
1 Tbsp. vegetable oil
2 Tbsp. skim milk
½ tsp. dried basil
2 Tbsp. plain dried bread crumbs
2 Tbsp. grated Parmesan cheese
⅛ tsp. salt
1 Tbsp. lemon juice

In a bowl, combine bread crumbs, cheese, salt and basil; mix. Dip chicken cutlets into milk, then into crumb mixture; coat evenly. In a skillet, heat oil; add chicken and brown on both sides or until chicken is tender. Pour lemon juice over chicken.

Per serving:
242 calories
57.2 mg cholesterol
347 mg sodium
3.5 gm saturated fat
13.8 gm fat

Exchanges per serving
½ bread
2 fat
3 meat

On the side A small dinner roll, green beans, steamed just until crisp-tender, a glass of milk, and fresh pineapple slices for dessert balance this meal nutritionally.

2 Tbsp. margarine
1½ lb. chicken thighs, skinned
1½ tsp. flour
2 tsp. Worcestershire sauce
1 tsp. dry mustard
¾ tsp. curry powder
1 tsp. light soy sauce

Preheat oven to 375°F. In a small saucepan, heat margarine; add remaining ingredients, except chicken. Stir constantly until mixture is thick and smooth. In a 9 x 9-inch baking dish, arrange chicken in single layer. Pour curry mixture over chicken. Bake for 35 to 40 minutes. Baste chicken occasionally with pan juices.

Per serving
302 calories
221 mg cholesterol
280 mg sodium
3.9 gm saturated fat
17.9 gm fat

Exchanges per serving
1 fat
3 meat

On the side A ½ cup of white rice, seasoned with a little fresh parsley, a vegetable course of cauliflower and broccoli florets, steamed just until tender and seasoned with lemon juice, and a peachy milk shake complete this meal nutritionally.

Curry Country Chicken

Nonstick cooking spray
3 lb. fryer chicken, skinned, cut up ½ cup onions, chopped
⅓ cup chopped green pepper
1 tsp. minced garlic
1 16-oz. can low-sodium stewed tomatoes
⅓ cup raisins
2 tsp. curry powder
¼ tsp. nutmeg
2 Tbsp. cold water
1 Tbsp. cornstarch
3 cups cooked rice

Spray a skillet with nonstick cooking spray. Brown chicken in skillet on all sides. Add onion, green pepper, and garlic. Stir in tomatoes, raisins, curry powder and nutmeg, and bring to a boil. Reduce heat and simmer for 30 to 35 minutes. Remove chicken. Skim excess fat from sauce. Combine water and corn-starch; stir into sauce and cook until thickened. Serve chicken and sauce over rice.

Per serving
340 calories
12.5 mg cholesterol
242 mg sodium
0.166 gm saturated fat
5.0 gm fat

Exchanges per serving
1 bread
3 meat
1 vegetable

On the side A glass of milk and a fresh fruit complete this hearty one-dish meal nutritionally.

1 cup whole wheat bread crumbs
1½ tsp. onion powder
¾ tsp. garlic powder
¾ tsp. paprika
1½ tsp. curry powder
¾ tsp. dry mustard
⅛ tsp. pepper
1 cup skim milk
⅛ tsp. Tabasco sauce
2½ lbs. drumsticks, skinless

Preheat oven to 375°F. Combine bread crumbs, onion powder, garlic powder, paprika, curry powder, mustard, and pepper. Place milk and Tabasco sauce in a shallow dish and soak drumsticks. Roll drumsticks in crumb mixture and place in a nonstick baking dish. Bake 25 to 30 minutes.

Per serving
256 calories
91 mg cholesterol
178 mg sodium
2.5 gm saturated fat
9.31 gm fat

Exchanges per serving
1 bread
2 meat

On the side Corn on the cob, a tossed salad with your favorite low-calorie dressing, a glass of milk, and a baked apple complete this meal deliciously and nutritionally.

Dijon Chicken

Serves 4 **295**

2 boneless, skinless chicken breasts
¼ tsp. black pepper
1 Tbsp. vegetable oil
1 Tbsp. margarine
¼ cup chopped fresh chives
1 Tbsp. lemon juice
1 tsp. dried parsley flakes
3 tsp. Dijon-style mustard
¼ cup low-sodium chicken broth

Sprinkle chicken with pepper. Heat oil and margarine in skillet. Cook chicken until browned and tender; do not over cook. Transfer to warm serving platter. Add chives, lemon juice, parsley, and mustard to skillet. Cook, stirring constantly for about 30 seconds. Stir in broth, stirring gently until smooth. Pour mixture over chicken and serve.

Per serving
230 calories
73 mg cholesterol
34 mg sodium
2.3 gm saturated fat
11.5 gm fat

Exchanges per serving
2½ meat

On the side We like to serve this with baked potato sticks, cherry tomatoes, quickly sautéed with a little margarine and sprinkled with basil, and a peachy milk shake. This completes the meal nutritionally and deliciously.

10 oz. skinned, boneless chicken breasts

1 tsp. margarine

6 broccoli florets

1 tsp. minced garlic

¾ tsp. ground ginger

⅔ cup low-sodium chicken broth

2½ Tbsp. oyster sauce

2 tsp. cornstarch

Cut chicken into strips. In skillet, heat margarine; add chicken and brown on both sides. Remove from skillet. In same skillet, add broccoli, garlic and ginger; sauté. In a mixing bowl, combine broth, oyster sauce, and cornstarch; add to broccoli and return chicken to skillet. Stir until sauce is thickened, then serve.

Per serving
426 calories
128 mg cholesterol
214 mg sodium
2.25 gm saturated fat
6.8 gm fat

Exchanges per serving
5 meat
1 vegetable

On the side A serving of brown rice, and frozen peaches, blended in a glass of nonfat milk, add the bread, fruit, and milk exchanges needed to make this meal nutritionally complete.

2 ½ lb. chicken, cut into parts, skinned
2 Tbsp. olive oil
2 garlic cloves, pressed
2 tsp. paprika
2 tsp. rosemary, crushed
⅛ tsp. pepper
⅛ tsp. salt

Preheat oven to 350°F. Rub each piece of chicken with olive oil and garlic. Mix paprika, rosemary, and pepper and salt together. Sprinkle mixture over each piece of chicken. Place in a baking dish and bake for 40 minutes or until chicken is done.

Per serving
354 calories
169 mg cholesterol
164 mg sodium
4.4 gm saturated fat
14 gm fat

Exchanges per serving
1 fat
4 meat

On the side Try this with baked potato slices, green beans and carrots, steamed just until crisp-tender, and a strawberry milk shake. We think you'll enjoy this meal, which is nutritionally complete as well as tasty.

⅓ cup long grain rice
1 cup sliced carrots
    ½ cup sliced green onions
    ½ tsp. minced garlic

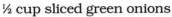
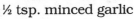

    ⅔ cup water
    3 Tbsp. soy sauce
    ¾ tsp. five-spice powder
⅛ tsp. pepper
1 whole chicken breast, skinless, halved

Preheat oven to 375°F. Cover a shallow casserole dish with heavy foil, cupping sides of foil. Place uncooked rice in middle. Add carrots, onions, and garlic. In a mixing bowl, combine water, soy sauce, five-spice powder and pepper. Place chicken breasts in center of foil. Pour soy sauce mixture over chicken. Fold two opposite sides of foil together, then fold up ends to seal. Bake for 50 minutes.

Per serving
240 calories
43 mg cholesterol
183 mg sodium
0.65 gm saturated fat
2.2 gm fat

Exchanges per serving
1 bread
2 meat
½ vegetable

On the side A small serving of green beans, steamed just until crisp-tender, a glass of milk, and a baked maple apple complete this meal nutritionally.

Fruited Chicken

1 tsp. salt
¼ tsp. pepper
¼ tsp. cinnamon
¼ tsp. ground cloves
1 tsp. minced garlic
2 3-lb. frying chickens, skinned,
    cut into serving-size pieces
2 Tbsp. vegetable oil
¼ cup chopped celery
¼ cup raisins
2 cups orange juice
¼ cup crushed pineapple, fresh
2 Tbsp. cornstarch
¼ cup water

Combine salt, pepper, cinnamon, cloves, and garlic.
Rub into chicken pieces. In skillet, heat oil; brown
chicken. Add celery, raisins, orange juice and pineapple. Cover and simmer 45 minutes or until chicken
is tender. Stir occasionally. Blend cornstarch and
water; stir into sauce. Cook, stirring until thickened.

Per serving
273 calories
89 mg cholesterol
377 mg sodium
2.5 gm saturated fat
7.5 gm fat

Exchanges per serving
1 fruit
3 meat

On the side A serving of white rice, a glass of milk, and your
choice of vegetable complete this meal nutritionally.

2 chicken breasts, boneless, skinned
1 can (16 oz.) peach halves
4 Tbsp. Dijon-style mustard
½ cup green onions, sliced
1 tsp. soy sauce
¾ cup dry bread crumbs

Preheat oven to 425°F. Place chicken in baking dish. Cover loosely with foil and bake for 25 minutes. Remove foil and place fruit on chicken. Combine mustard, onion, and soy sauce, and spread over chicken. Sprinkle with bread crumbs. Broil until brown.

Per serving
375 calories
85 mg cholesterol
486 mg sodium
1.6 gm saturated fat
6.3 gm fat

Exchanges per serving
1 bread
1 fruit
3 meat

On the side A traditional spinach salad goes well on the side with this tasty main dish. Add only a glass of milk and the meal is complete nutritionally.

Ginger-Glazed Chicken

2½ lbs. skinned frying chicken
⅔ cup low-cal ginger marmalade
1 Tbsp. ginger flavored brandy
1 Tbsp. oil
4 Tbsp. lime juice

Preheat oven to 375°F. Arrange chicken in a large shallow pan. Combine marmalade, brandy, oil and lime juice. Brush on chicken pieces. Bake for 40 minutes. Baste frequently.

Per serving
280 calories
78 mg cholesterol
75 mg sodium
3.2 gm saturated fat
12.8 gm fat

Exchanges per serving
½ fat
4 meat

On the side Brown rice, green beans, steamed just until crisp-tender, a glass of milk, and your favorite fruit for dessert combine to make this meal nutritionally complete.

302 Glazed Chicken

Serves 4

2 boned, skinned chicken breasts, halved
¼ cup plain low-fat yogurt
3 tsp. brown sugar
3 tsp. Worcestershire sauce
1 Tbsp. minced garlic
⅛ tsp. black pepper
⅛ tsp. Tabasco sauce

Preheat oven to 350°F. In bowl, combine all ingredients, except chicken. Mix well. In shallow baking dish, arrange chicken. Pour half of yogurt mixture over chicken and bake for about 25 minutes or until chicken is tender. Pour remaining yogurt mixture over chicken and broil until lightly brown.

Per serving
188 calories
72 mg cholesterol
189 mg sodium
1.75 gm saturated fat
6.1 gm fat

Exchanges per serving
2 meat

On the side A serving of white rice, lightly sautéed snow pea pods, a glass of milk, and pears garnished with a little mint combine to make this meal nutritionally balanced.

4 whole chicken breasts, boned, skinned, halved
¼ cup margarine
⅓ cup honey
4 Tbsp. Dijon-style mustard
1 tsp. minced garlic
1 Tbsp. lemon juice
2 tsp. curry powder
⅛ tsp. salt

Preheat oven to 350°F. Arrange chicken in a 13 x 9-inch baking dish. Melt margarine in a saucepan; add remaining ingredients and stir until smooth. Pour over chicken. Cook for 25 to 30 minutes, basting frequently.

Per serving
242 calories
73 mg cholesterol
136 mg sodium
2.6 gm saturated fat
6.7 gm fat

Exchanges per serving
1 fat
3 meat

On the side Saffron rice, sautéed onions, mushrooms, and green peppers, a glass of milk, and your favorite fruit for dessert finish off this tasty dish and make the meal complete nutritionally.

Serves 4

6 5-oz. boneless, skinless chicken breasts
3 tsp. Dijon mustard
¼ cup white wine vinegar
5 tsp. minced garlic
2 Tbsp. honey
1 tsp. dried thyme
¼ tsp. salt
¼ tsp. crushed red pepper flakes
1 Tbsp. light extra virgin olive oil
Nonstick cooking spray

Place breasts in a shallow glass dish. Combine mustard, vinegar, garlic, honey, thyme, salt, and pepper in a small bowl and stir. Add oil and whisk to combine. Pour over chicken breast and marinate in refrigerator for 3 hours. Lightly grease grill with cooking spray. Remove breasts from marinade and place on grill. Baste frequently with marinade until breasts are tender and cooked.

Per serving
308 calories
99 mg cholesterol
312 mg sodium
3 gm saturated fat
12.7 gm fat

Exchanges per serving
4 meat
1 fat

On the side A mixed green salad, a glass of milk, and fresh fruit for dessert complete this meal nutritiously.

8 chicken breast halves without skin
¼ cup lemon juice
½ cup lime juice
⅓ cup olive oil
4 chopped green onions
4 minced garlic cloves
3 Tbsp. chopped fresh dill, divided
¼ tsp. pepper

Pound chicken breasts to flatten. Combine lemon juice, lime juice, oil, onions, garlic, 2 tablespoons dill and pepper in a resealable plastic bag. Add chicken; seal, refrigerate 2 to 4 hours. Drain, discard marinade. Grill chicken, uncovered, over medium hot coals for 12 to 15 minutes, until tender and juices run clear. Turn after 6 minutes. Sprinkle with remaining dill before serving.

Per serving
235 calories
65 mg cholesterol
87 mg sodium
3.4 gm saturated fat
16.6 gm fat

Exchanges per serving
4 meat
2 fat

On the side Serve with brown rice, steamed broccoli, fresh fruit and a glass of milk to make this meal complete.

2 boneless, skinless chicken breasts, cut into chunks
¾ cup chopped green peppers
1 8-oz. can pineapple chunks
   in unsweetened juice
1 Tbsp. lemon juice
¼ tsp. paprika
4 cups cooked rice

In saucepan, add chicken, green peppers, and pineapple with its juice. Heat to boil. Simmer and add lemon juice and paprika. Cook until chicken is tender. Serve over rice.

Per serving
271 calories
425 mg cholesterol
491 mg sodium
0.65 gm saturated fat
2.25 gm fat

Exchanges per serving
1 bread
½ fruit
2 meat

On the side Serve this with a tossed salad and a cherry milk shake and the meal is complete nutritionally.

3½ lb. chicken, cut into pieces, skinned
2 Tbsp. vegetable oil
½ tsp. garlic powder
½ tsp. onion powder or salt
½ tsp. pepper
2 tsp. oregano
2 tsp. basil
2 tsp. lime juice
1½ cups chopped fresh tomato

Preheat oven to 450°F. Rub chicken pieces first with vegetable oil, then with garlic powder, onion powder, pepper, oregano, and basil. Place chicken in oven-proof casserole dish. Sprinkle with lime juice. Bake chicken for 20 to 25 minutes. Reduce heat to 350°F. Add tomatoes to the chicken and bake for an additional 20 to 25 minutes.

Per serving
310 calories
178 mg cholesterol
174 mg sodium
4.4 gm saturated fat
15 gm fat

Exchanges per serving
1 fat
3 meat
1 vegetable

On the side We like to serve this with a baked potato, a vegetable mix of cauliflower florets and carrots, a glass of milk, and fresh fruit for dessert. The meal is nutritionally complete and completely satisfying.

308 Honey and Mustard Chicken

1 whole chicken, cut up
½ cup honey
½ cup margarine, melted
2 tsp. dry mustard

Preheat oven to 350°F. Rinse chicken and pat dry. Combine honey, margarine and mustard; mix. Put chicken in baking dish. Brush honey mixture on chicken. Bake for 1 hour. Baste occasionally with mixture.

Per serving
220 calories
73 mg cholesterol
138 mg sodium
2.6 gm saturated fat
7.16 gm fat

Exchanges per serving
½ fat
1½ meat

On the side Parsley potatoes, baby carrots, simmered with gingerroot, a glass of milk, and mixed fruit slices for dessert complete this meal deliciously and nutritiously.

2 boned, skinned chicken breasts, halved
1 Tbsp. margarine, melted
¼ tsp. garlic powder
¼ cup lime juice
5 tsp. honey
3 tsp. Dijon-style mustard

Heat oven to 350°F. In nonstick baking dish, place chicken. Baste chicken with margarine and sprinkle with garlic powder. Bake for about 25 to 30 minutes. In saucepan, combine lime juice, honey, and mustard; heat. Spread mixture over chicken. Broil chicken until lightly brown.

Per serving
212 calories
71 mg cholesterol
93 mg sodium
2.1 gm saturated fat
7.6 gm fat

Exchanges per serving
2 meat

On the side We like to serve white rice, a mixed vegetable of green beans and carrots, a glass of milk, and a compote of mixed melon balls with this tangy entree. The meal is nutritionally complete and satisfying to the eye and the palate.

½ cup chopped onion
½ tsp. minced garlic
½ cup green pepper
2 cups skinned and cooked chicken, cubed
1 Tbsp. vegetable oil
½ tsp. black pepper
1½ tsp. curry powder
1 28 oz. can stewed tomatoes
1 Tbsp. Worcestershire sauce
¼ cup raisins
2 cups cooked rice

In large skillet, heat oil. Add onions, garlic, and green pepper; sauté until onions are tender. Add the remaining ingredients, except the rice. Simmer for 30 minutes. Serve over the rice.

Per serving
323 calories
71 mg cholesterol
930 mg sodium
1.91 gm saturated fat
8.3 gm fat

Exchanges
1 bread
2½ meat
1 vegetable

On the side This meal is nearly complete in one dish. Serve with a dessert of fruit and yogurt for nutritional balance.

Lemon-Barbecued Chicken

2½ lb. frying chicken, quartered and skinned
⅛ tsp. paprika
⅛ tsp. cayenne pepper
¼ cup lemon juice
¼ cup honey

Season chicken with paprika and pepper. Place chicken on broiler rack. Combine lemon juice and honey; mix thoroughly. Baste chicken with lemon-honey mixture. Broil 15 minutes; baste occasionally with lemon-honey mixture. Turn pieces over and baste. Broil until chicken is done.

Per serving
300 calories
247.5 mg cholesterol
192.5 mg sodium
3.24 gm saturated fat
11.5 gm fat

Exchanges per serving
4 meat

On the side Corn on the cob, a tossed salad, a glass of milk, and a slice of watermelon for dessert make this a picnic any time of the year. The meal is nutritionally complete and is sure to please the entire family.

312 Lemon Chicken Sauté

Serves 4

Nonstick cooking spray
2 large skinless chicken breasts cut in half
⅛ tsp. salt
⅛ tsp. pepper
½ cup chopped green onions
1 Tbsp. dried parsley flakes, crushed
¾ tsp. marjoram
½ cup lemon juice

Spray skillet with cooking spray. Sprinkle chicken with salt and pepper, and brown on all sides. Sprinkle chicken with onions, parsley, and marjoram. Pour lemon juice over chicken, cover and simmer 20 to 25 minutes

Per serving
200 calories
99 mg cholesterol
181 mg sodium
2.3 gm saturated fat
8.3 gm fat

Exchanges per serving
4 meat

On the side We like this entrée with brown rice, cooked cabbage, and a cherry milkshake.

One Year of Healthy, Hearty & Simple One-Dish Meals

Low-Fat Chicken Stroganoff

Nonstick cooking spray
1 lb. chicken breast skinned, cubed
1 cup chopped onions
½ tsp. crushed garlic
2½ cups low-sodium chicken broth
2½ Tbsp. flour
¾ cup dry red wine
2 cups sliced mushrooms
1 cup light sour cream

Spray skillet with cooking spray. Brown chicken, onion, and garlic. Add chicken broth; cover and simmer until chicken is cooked thoroughly. Dissolve flour in wine, then whisk into meat juices until thickened. Add mushrooms and simmer for 5 to 10 minutes. Add sour cream and simmer an additional 5 to 10 minutes.

Per serving
219 calories
38 mg cholesterol
339 mg sodium
1.1 gm saturated fat
12 gm fat

Exchanges per serving
1½ meat
1½ fat
½ vegetable

On the side This tasty Stroganoff is delicious over fettuccine noodles (½ cup per serving). A side salad, a glass of milk, and fruit for dessert make the meal complete nutritionally.

1 Tbsp. vegetable oil

4 boneless, skinless chicken breasts, halved

1 Tbsp. margarine

⅔ cup diced onions

¾ cup low-sodium canned tomatoes

¾ tsp. basil

⅛ tsp. garlic powder

¼ tsp. thyme

¼ cup sweet vermouth

In skillet, heat oil and brown chicken on both sides. Transfer chicken to a large saucepan. Melt margarine in same skillet and sauté onions. Add to chicken in saucepan. Add remaining ingredients to saucepan and simmer for 30 minutes.

Per serving
219 calories
83 mg cholesterol
28 mg sodium
1.4 gm saturated fat
3.75 gm fat

Exchanges per serving
3 meat

On the side A serving of white rice; sautéed onions, mushrooms, and green peppers, sautéed, a glass of milk, and a pear poached in almond extract complete this meal nutritionally and make it deliciously appealing, as well.

Moist Turkey Loaf

1 lb. ground turkey
⅔ cup oatmeal
½ cup skim milk
1 egg
⅓ cup chopped onions
1 Tbsp. mustard
1 Tbsp. Worcestershire sauce
½ tsp. black pepper
¼ cup ketchup

Preheat oven to 350°F. In a large bowl, mix all the ingredients together; blend well. Shape into a loaf and place in a loaf pan. Bake for 1½ hours.

Per serving
122 calories
53 mg cholesterol
270 mg sodium
1.2 gm saturated fat
4.7 gm fat

Exchanges per serving
1 meat

On the side Onions, mushrooms, and green peppers, sautéed in a little margarine, a glass of milk, and baked apple dessert complete this meal nutritionally.

1 Tbsp. margarine
1 cup sliced mushrooms
1½ Tbsp. light cream cheese
¼ tsp. nutmeg
1 Tbsp. minced green onion
⅛ tsp. ground pepper
1 chicken breast, skinned, boned, halved
¼ cup balsamic vinegar

Preheat oven to 350°F. In skillet, heat margarine. Add mushrooms and sauté until liquid is absorbed. Mash cream cheese with nutmeg, green onion, and pepper. Spoon half of the mushroom mixture on each piece of chicken. Put half the cream cheese on top, then loosely fold chicken sides to middle. Place chicken in a casserole dish, seam side down. Pour vinegar over chicken. Bake uncovered for 30 minutes.

Per serving
174 calories
51 mg cholesterol
173 mg sodium
2.7 gm saturated fat
9.2 gm fat

Exchanges per serving
2 meat
1 vegetable

On the side Green noodles, baby carrots cooked with a little mint, and a dessert of fruit slices, sprinkled with poppy seeds, and served with a yogurt dip complete this meal nutritionally and give it a little touch of elegance well suited for guests.

Mustard-Coated Chicken

3 Tbsp. Dijon-style mustard
⅔ cup plain bread crumbs
1½ Tbsp. lime juice
5 Tbsp. water
12 oz. boneless, skinless chicken breasts
1 Tbsp. vegetable oil
2 Tbsp. dry white wine

Mix together mustard, bread crumbs, lime juice and water to make a paste. Put half of the mustard coating on one side of each chicken breast. In a skillet, heat oil. Place coated side of chicken in pan. While breasts are sautéing, spread remaining coating on top; brown both sides. Reduce heat and add wine; cook another 5 minutes.

Per serving
299 calories
71 mg cholesterol
245 mg sodium
3.3 gm saturated fat
8 gm fat

Exchanges per serving
4 meat

On the side Parsley new potatoes, fresh tomato slices, a glass of milk, and your favorite fruit for dessert complete this meal nutritionally.

1 Tbsp. vegetable oil
1 lb. chicken breasts, boneless, skinned
1 cup chopped green pepper
¼ cup chopped green onion
1 tsp. minced garlic
1 cup orange juice
1½ tsp. dry mustard
⅛ tsp. salt
⅛ tsp. pepper
3 tsp. cornstarch, dissolved in 3 Tbsp. water
1 small orange, cut into small pieces
⅛ tsp. ginger

Heat oil in skillet. Add chicken and brown; remove. In same skillet, add green pepper, green onion, and garlic. Cook until tender. Return chicken to skillet. Add orange juice, mustard, salt and pepper, and bring to a boil. Reduce heat and simmer for 15 minutes. Transfer chicken to platter; keep warm. Add cornstarch mixture to skillet. Increase heat. Add orange pieces and cook until thickened. Pour over chicken. Sprinkle lightly with ginger.

Per serving
268 calories
97 mg cholesterol
164 mg sodium
1.9 gm saturated fat
8.6 gm fat

Exchanges per serving
1 fat
½ fruit
2 meat
1 vegetable

On the side We prefer white rice and cooked fresh spinach with this delightful entree. Top off the meal with a cherry milk shake for nutritional balance.

Orange-Glazed Chicken

1 lb. skinned, boned chicken breasts
⅓ cup low-calorie orange spread
¼ cup light soy sauce
¾ tsp. ground ginger
¼ tsp. garlic powder

In mixing bowl, combine all ingredients, except chicken; mix well. Cut chicken into large cubes. Put chicken in mixture and toss to coat. Marinate in refrigerator for 30 minutes. Transfer chicken to broiling pan. Broil and baste, turning chicken until done.

Per serving
240 calories
85 mg cholesterol
906 mg sodium
1.3 gm saturated fat
4.5 gm fat

Exchanges per serving
2 meat

On the side Wild rice is really nice with this citrus-glazed chicken dish. Steamed broccoli and a dessert of fruit and yogurt complete the meal nutritionally.

320 Oriental Broiled Chicken

¾ cup orange juice

¼ cup honey

4 Tbsp. soy sauce

½ tsp. minced garlic

⅛ tsp. ginger

3 lb. broiling chicken, quartered, skinned

Combine orange juice, honey, soy sauce, garlic and ginger. Stir until honey is dissolved. Arrange chicken on a broiling pan. Pour half of orange juice mixture over chicken. Broil for 5 minutes. Turn chicken over and pour remaining mixture over chicken. Broil until chicken is tender.

Per serving
300 calories
153 mg cholesterol
561 mg sodium
3.4 gm saturated fat
12.6 gm fat

Exchanges per serving
3 meat

On the side White rice, snow pea pods, a glass of milk, and your favorite fresh fruit for dessert are all you need to complete this meal nutritionally.

Oven-Baked Barbecued Chicken Serves 6 **321**

3 lbs. chicken, skinned
2 cups tomato juice
¾ cup vinegar
2 Tbsp. Worcestershire sauce
2 Tbsp. brown sugar
⅛ tsp. salt
¼ tsp. dry mustard
½ tsp. ground red pepper
⅛ tsp. pepper
1 Tbsp. minced onion
1 tsp. ketchup

Preheat oven to 350°F. In a saucepan, combine all ingredients except chicken. Cook over medium heat, stirring frequently for about 10 minutes. In a 13 x 9-inch baking dish, arrange chicken in an even layer; top with tomato mixture. Bake, basting chicken frequently for 55 minutes.

Per serving
325 calories
212 mg cholesterol
323 mg sodium
4.57 gm saturated fat
12.9 gm fat

Exchanges per serving
4 meat
1 vegetable

On the side New potatoes garnished with rosemary, a glass of milk, and fresh strawberries for dessert complete this meal nutritionally.

Nonstick cooking spray
8 boneless skinless chicken breast halves
1 cup fat-free mayonnaise
½ cup grated Parmesan cheese
2 tsp. dried oregano
⅛ tsp. pepper
¼ tsp. paprika

Preheat oven to 400°F. Place chicken in a shallow
3-quart baking dish that has been coated with
cooking spray. Bake, uncovered, for 20 minutes.
Combine mayonnaise, cheese, oregano, and pepper;
spread over chicken. Sprinkle with paprika. Bake 20
minutes more or until chicken juices run clear.

Per serving
252 calories
101 mg cholesterol
337 mg sodium
4.2 gm saturated fat
11.2 gm fat

Exchanges per serving
4 meat

On the side Serve with a baked potato, mixed vegetables and
fresh fruit round out the meal nutritionally.

Paprika Chicken

1 Tbsp. vegetable oil
1 cup chopped onions
½ tsp. minced garlic
4 tsp. paprika
⅛ tsp. black pepper
1½ cups low-sodium chicken broth
1½ Tbsp. cornstarch
2 cups skinned and cooked chicken, cubed
⅔ cup frozen peas
1 cup plain low-fat yogurt
2½ cups cooked noodles

In a large skillet, heat oil. Sauté onions, garlic, paprika, and pepper. Cook until onions are tender. Add broth and cornstarch; stir until smooth. Bring to a boil and add chicken and peas. Boil for 1 minute. Remove from heat and stir in yogurt until blended. Serve over noodles.

Per serving
345 calories
100 mg cholesterol
250 mg sodium
2.21 gm saturated fat
9.6 gm fat

Exchanges per serving
1 bread
1 fat
3 meat

On the side This main-dish meal goes well with a mixed vegetable of green beans and carrots, a glass of milk, and your favorite fruit for dessert.

2 lbs. chicken, skinned
6 Tbsp. margarine
1 cup chopped onions
2 cups fresh, sliced mushrooms
1 cup chopped celery
4 Tbsp. flour
1 cup low-sodium chicken broth
1 cup skim milk
1 tsp. celery salt
1 tsp. dried tarragon

Preheat oven to 400°F. Cut chicken into serving
pieces. Place in shallow pan and bake for 15 minutes.
Baste with 3 Tbsp. melted margarine and continue
baking for 15 minutes longer. Transfer chicken to a
casserole dish and set aside. In skillet, heat remaining
3 tablespoons margarine. Sauté onions, mushrooms
and celery until soft. Put over chicken, leaving pan
drippings. Add flour, chicken broth, and milk to pan
drippings, stirring constantly until sauce thickens.
Remove from heat and season with celery salt and
tarragon. Pour over chicken and bake at 350°F for
20 minutes.

Per serving
290 calories
70 mg cholesterol
114 mg sodium
2.0 gm saturated fat
12.0 gm fat

Exchanges per serving
1 fat
3 meat
1 vegetable

On the side We like this tasty casserole with a side of saffron rice,
a glass of milk, and, if they are in season, some honeydew and
cantaloupe melon slices for dessert.

Quick and Easy Chicken

2 Tbsp. margarine
2 boneless, skinned chicken breasts
¼ tsp. salt
¼ tsp. black pepper
1 lemon

In skillet, melt margarine. Sprinkle chicken with salt and pepper. Brown chicken on each side. Cook until chicken is done. Squeeze lemon over chicken. Simmer for about 2 minutes. Serve.

Per serving
220 calories
73 mg cholesterol
133 mg sodium
2.41 gm saturated fat
11.3 gm fat

Exchanges per serving
1 fat
2½ meat

On the side Our favorite accompaniments are green noodles, cooked carrots, and a strawberry milk shake with this quick and easy recipe. They give the meal an appealing appearance to the eye as well as appealing to the palate.

1 Tbsp. Dijon-style mustard
2 tsp. light mayonnaise
2 tsp. plain low-fat yogurt
2 chicken breasts, skinned
1½ cups fine bread crumbs

Preheat oven to 350°F. Mix mustard, mayonnaise, and yogurt. Spread mixture over both sides of chicken breasts; dredge in bread crumbs. Place in a baking dish and cover. Bake for 35 minutes.

Per serving
364 calories
86 mg cholesterol
666 mg sodium
2.1 gm saturated fat
8.8 gm fat

Exchanges per serving
1 bread
1 fat
3 meat

On the side Cherry tomatoes, lightly sautéed with a little margarine and basil, are delicious with this Quick Baked Chicken recipe. Add a glass of milk and your favorite fruit for dessert and the meal is nutritionally complete.

Riced Chicken

1½ cups crisp rice cereal, crushed
1 6-oz. envelope Italian salad dressing mix
1 tsp. basil
4 large skinless chicken breast, cut in halves
¼ cup margarine, melted

Preheat oven to 375°F. In mixing bowl, combine
cereal, salad dressing mix, and basil. Brush chicken
with melted margarine, then roll in cereal mixture.
Place chicken in shallow baking pan. Sprinkle with
any remaining crumbs. Bake for 50 minutes.

Per serving
324 calories
80 mg cholesterol
3055 mg sodium
3.4 gm saturated fat
13.8 gm fat

Exchanges per serving
1 fat
4 meat

On the side A mix of cauliflower and broccoli florets, steamed
just until tender, a glass of milk, and your favorite fruit
complete this meal nutritionally.

1 Tbsp. vegetable oil
1 Tbsp. margarine
1 tsp. minced garlic
2 Tbsp. lemon juice
¼ tsp. nutmeg
3 lb. chicken
2 potatoes, quartered

Preheat oven to 350°F. In skillet, heat oil and margarine until foamy. Add garlic, lemon juice, and nutmeg. Add chicken to pan, breast side up. Brush with basting mixture. Place chicken in shallow baking dish. Place potatoes around chicken. Bake for 35 to 40 minutes. Baste occasionally.

Per serving
409 calories
153 mg cholesterol
169 mg sodium
3.9 gm saturated fat
16.0 gm fat

Exchanges per serving
½ bread
1 fat
3 meat

On the side Choose your favorite vegetable to accompany this classic roast chicken dish. A glass of milk and some baked apple slices for dessert complete the meal nutritionally.

Roasted Chicken

2 lbs. whole chicken, skinned
1 tsp. dried thyme
⅛ tsp. pepper
⅓ cup water
¾ cup sliced onion
2 cups frozen brussel sprouts
2 Tbsp. honey

Preheat oven to 350°F. Sprinkle chicken with thyme
and pepper. Place chicken in a baking dish. Add water
to baking dish and top chicken with onions. Cover
and bake about 20 to 25 minutes. Add brussel
sprouts around chicken. Drizzle honey over chicken
and continue to bake for 20 to 25 minutes longer.

Per serving
336 calories
136 mg cholesterol
140 mg sodium
3.0 gm saturated fat
11.3 gm fat

Exchanges per serving
4 meat
1 vegetable

On the side A baked potato, a side salad, a glass of milk, and
fresh fruit for dessert complete this classic meal nutritionally.

2 lbs. chicken breasts, skinned
1 can cream of mushroom soup
¾ cup skim milk
¼ cup sliced onion
1 tsp. dried rosemary, crushed
2 cups fresh mushrooms
½ tsp. dried thyme
⅛ tsp. pepper

Preheat oven to 350°F. Place chicken in baking dish. In saucepan, add remaining ingredients. Mix well and heat for 10 minutes. Pour mixture over chicken. Cover and bake for 40 to 45 minutes.

Per serving
351 calories
131 mg cholesterol
483 mg sodium
3.8 gm saturated fat
11.6 gm fat

Exchanges per serving
1 fat
3 meat

On the side New potatoes, boiled, then tossed in a pan with a little margarine and some rosemary, a green vegetable of broccoli or green beans, and a frozen fruit yogurt dessert complete this meal deliciously and nutritionally.

Saucy Chicken

6 oz. jar artichoke hearts, drained
2 tsp. cornstarch
¾ tsp. instant chicken bouillon
⅛ tsp. salt
⅛ tsp. pepper
⅔ cup skim milk
1 cup cubed cooked chicken
3 Tbsp. grated Parmesan cheese
¼ tsp. paprika

Preheat oven to 350°F. Cut artichokes into small pieces; rinse and drain in hot water. In a saucepan, combine cornstarch, chicken bouillon, salt and pepper. Stir in skim milk and cook over medium heat until thickened. Stir in cubed chicken and artichoke hearts. Transfer mixture into a casserole dish. Sprinkle with Parmesan cheese and paprika. Bake, uncovered, for 15 minutes.

Per serving
328 calories
115 mg cholesterol
770 mg sodium
3.9 gm saturated fat
11.8 gm fat

Exchanges per serving
2 meat
½ skim milk
1 vegetable

On the side Wild rice is great with this robust recipe. Prepare a dessert plate of fruit slices, sprinkled with poppy seeds, accompanied by a yogurt dip and the meal is nutritionally complete.

332 Scotch Chicken

2 boneless chicken breasts
⅛ tsp. salt
⅛ tsp. ground pepper
1 Tbsp. Scotch whiskey
⅓ cup low-sodium chicken broth
1 cup sliced mushrooms
2 tsp. skim milk
1 Tbsp. low-fat cottage cheese
1 Tbsp. low-fat yogurt
⅛ tsp. nutmeg

Season chicken with salt and pepper and place in a nonstick skillet, skin side down. Sear, covered, over high heat for 3 to 4 minutes. Turn chicken over and reduce heat and cook for another 3 to 4 minutes. Remove chicken. Deglaze skillet with Scotch. Reduce liquid until it's just a film; stir constantly. Add broth and mushrooms, cover and boil, stirring occasionally. Remove from heat. Stir in milk, cottage cheese, and yogurt. Season with nutmeg. Pour over chicken.

Per serving
195 calories
42.5 mg cholesterol
672 mg sodium
2.1 gm saturated fat
5.4 gm fat

Exchanges per serving
3 meat
½ vegetable

On the side Saffron rice, green beans, seasoned with garlic, a glass of milk and your favorite fruit for dessert combine to complete this meal nutritionally.

Spanish Chicken Bake

1⅓ cups water
4½ oz. package Spanish-style rice mix
¾ cup sliced mushrooms
¼ cup diced green chili peppers
4 boneless, skinless chicken breast halves
½ cup shredded part-skim cheddar cheese

Preheat oven to 350°F. Boil water. In baking dish, combine water and rice mixture. Stir mushrooms and chili peppers into rice mixture. Arrange chicken on top of rice mixture and cover with foil. Bake for 40 minutes. Sprinkle with cheese, then bake uncovered until cheese melts.

Per serving
276 calories
86 mg cholesterol
197 mg sodium
1.5 gm saturated fat
6.2 gm fat

Exchanges per serving
½ bread
3 meat

On the side A salad of lettuce and tomatoes, a glass of milk, and a dessert of baked maple apples complete this meal deliciously and nutritionally.

¾ tsp. oregano
¾ tsp. ginger
⅓ cup cornmeal

¾ tsp. basil
1 tsp. minced garlic
½ tsp. lemon juice
4 chicken cutlets, skinned
1 egg white, beaten lightly
½ tsp. Tabasco sauce
½ cup bran flakes, crushed

Preheat oven to 350°F. Combine oregano, ginger, cornmeal, basil, and garlic. Rub lemon juice on chicken cutlets. Mix egg white and Tabasco. Dip chicken in cornmeal mixture, then in egg white mixture; then roll in bran flakes. Place chicken on nonstick baking sheet. Bake for 20 to 25 minutes.

Per serving
200 calories
21 mg cholesterol
274 mg sodium
1.0 gm saturated fat
2.8 gm fat

Exchanges per serving
½ bread
2 meat

On the side White rice, steamed broccoli florets, and a strawberry milk shake complete this meal nutritionally.

Spicy Chicken

Serves 4 **335**

Nonstick cooking spray
2 boneless, skinless chicken breasts
4 Tbsp. sugar
4 Tbsp. lemon juice
2 tsp. Worcestershire sauce
1 tsp. paprika
½ tsp. black pepper
½ tsp. lemon pepper
½ tsp. salt

Spray broiler pan with nonstick spray. Place chicken on pan. Combine all ingredients and mix well. Brush chicken with sauce. Broil, turning chicken and basting with sauce until chicken is done.

Per serving
213 calories
73 mg cholesterol
627 mg sodium
1.41 gm saturated fat
5.3 gm fat

Exchanges per serving
3 meat

On the side Parsley new potatoes, green beans, a glass of milk, and some fresh pineapple slices for dessert are all you need to complete this meal deliciously and nutritionally.

2 lbs. chicken pieces, skinless
1 cup cornflake crumbs
2 tsp. chili powder
½ tsp. ground cumin
¼ tsp. ground red pepper
⅛ tsp. black pepper
¼ tsp. garlic powder

Preheat oven to 375°F. In shallow dish, combine all ingredients except chicken. Rinse chicken with water, then roll pieces in the crumb mixture to coat. Place chicken in nonstick baking pan. Bake 45 minutes.

Per serving
225 calories
100 mg cholesterol
200 mg sodium
1.6 gm saturated fat
5.5 gm fat

Exchanges per serving
3 meat

On the side Serve this spicy dish with a side of white rice, a serving of green beans, and a cherry milk shake for nutritional completeness and to get raves from the entire family.

Stir-Fry Chicken

2 boneless, skinned chicken breasts
2 Tbsp. cornstarch
3 Tbsp. soy sauce
¼ cup chopped green onions
½ cup chopped green pepper
½ cup chopped red pepper
1 cup sliced, fresh mushrooms
1 Tbsp. vegetable oil
½ cup low-sodium chicken broth
6 oz. package frozen pea pods, thawed
½ cup chopped tomatoes
4 cups cooked rice

Cut chicken into chunks. In bowl, combine chicken, cornstarch, and soy sauce. Over medium heat, cook onions, green pepper, red pepper, and mushrooms in oil until crisp-tender. Remove to a bowl. In a skillet, cook chicken mixture, stirring frequently. Add broth, pea pods, and vegetables from bowl. Cook until chicken is tender. Stir in tomatoes. Heat through, then serve with rice.

Per serving
287 calories
26 mg cholesterol
245.7 mg sodium
4 gm saturated fat
10 gm fat

Exchanges per serving
1 bread
2½ meat
1 vegetable

On the side This meal needs only a glass of milk and your favorite fruit as dessert to be complete nutritionally.

338 Stuffed Chicken

Serves 2

1 whole chicken breast, skinned, halved
4 Tbsp. soy sauce
2 Tbsp. margarine
2 tsp. lemon juice
1/2 tsp. thyme
1/8 tsp. pepper
1/4 tsp. grated lemon rind
4 Tbsp. grated part-skim Swiss cheese
1/2 tsp. dried parsley flakes

Preheat oven to 375°F. Cut a 2-inch pocket lengthwise on each side of chicken breast. In a saucepan,
combine soy sauce, margarine, lemon juice, thyme,
pepper, and lemon rind; bring to a boil. Place chicken
in a baking dish. Pour sauce over chicken and bake
for 25 to 30 minutes. Remove from oven. Divide
cheese and insert into the pockets in the chicken.
Return chicken to oven and bake until cheese melts.
Sprinkle with parsley.

Per serving
360 calories
91 mg cholesterol
2290 mg sodium
5.9 gm saturated fat
21.5 gm fat

Exchanges per serving
2 fat
4 meat

On the side Our preference is for green noodles as the bread
course, a tossed salad as the vegetable, a glass of milk, and a
mixed fruit salad of apple, peach, orange, and grapes for
dessert. This completes the meal nutritionally.

Supreme Chicken

1 whole chicken breast, halved, skinned
⅛ tsp. salt
⅛ tsp. pepper
2 Tbsp. margarine
2 cups sliced mushrooms
1¼ cup skim milk
1½ Tbsp. cornstarch
1 Tbsp. sherry

Preheat oven to 350°F. Sprinkle chicken with salt and pepper. Place in a baking dish. Dot each with one tablespoon margarine. Bake for 20 minutes. Add mushrooms and bake for 5 to 10 minutes longer. In a saucepan, blend milk and cornstarch until smooth; bring to a boil. Stir in sherry. Pour over chicken. Bake for 5 to 10 minutes more.

Per serving
293 calories
37 mg cholesterol
396 mg sodium
2.9 gm saturated fat
15.1 gm fat

Exchanges per serving
1 fat
2 meat
1 vegetable
½ skim milk

On the side Try this with parsley new potatoes, stir-fried zucchini with tomatoes and a plate of mixed fruit sticks with yogurt dip for a delicious and nutritionally complete meal.

1 large chicken breast, halved, skinned, and boned
1 egg, slightly beaten
3 Tbsp. flour
2 tsp. sesame seeds
¾ tsp. ground ginger
⅛ tsp. cinnamon
1 peach, sliced
⅛ cup sliced green onions
1 Tbsp. vegetable oil
¼ cup ketchup
3 Tbsp. wine vinegar
2½ tsp. brown sugar
2 tsp. soy sauce
½ tsp. minced garlic
1½ Tbsp. white wine

Cut breast into chunks. Combine egg, flour, sesame seed, ginger and cinnamon. Coat chicken with mixture. Heat oil in a skillet and cook chicken. Combine in a blender: ketchup, vinegar, brown sugar, soy sauce, garlic, and wine; blend. Stir in peach. Add sauce and onions to chicken and cook for 5 to 10 minutes.

Per serving
327 calories
168 mg cholesterol
704 mg sodium
2.4 gm saturated fat
12.5 gm fat

Exchanges per serving
1 fat
½ fruit
3 meat

On the side A serving of white rice, a side of green beans, steamed just until crisp, a glass of milk, and a pineapple slice on the plate as garnish round out this meal.

Swiss Chicken

1 10-oz. package frozen spinach
4 boned, skinless chicken breast halves
⅔ cup skim milk
1½ tsp. cornstarch
2 tsp. instant chicken bouillon granules
¾ tsp. caraway seed
⅛ tsp. paprika
⅓ cup shredded part-skim Swiss cheese

Cook spinach according to package directions; drain.
In a nonstick skillet, cook chicken over medium heat,
turning occasionally, until tender. Place spinach in a
baking dish and place chicken atop spinach. For
sauce, combine milk, cornstarch, bouillon, caraway
seed and paprika. Cook and stir until thickened and
bubbly. Add cheese and stir until melted. Pour sauce
over chicken and bake at 375°F for 10 minutes.

Per serving
254 calories
79 mg. cholesterol
643 mg sodium
1.5 gm saturated fat
9 gm fat

Exchanges per serving
3 meat
1 vegetable

On the side New potatoes, boiled, then tossed in a little
margarine and parsley, are great beside this tasty chicken and
spinach mix. Add a glass of milk and your favorite fresh fruit
for dessert and the meal is nutritionally complete.

342 Tangy Chicken

3 Tbsp. minced onion
2 tsp. minced garlic
½ tsp. ground ginger
2 cups low-fat yogurt
½ tsp. coriander
¼ tsp. cumin
1 Tbsp. Worcestershire sauce
½ Tbsp. soy sauce
¼ cup lime juice
⅓ cup orange juice
¾ tsp. paprika
4 whole skinless, boned chicken breasts, halved

Mix onion, garlic and ginger in a bowl. Add yogurt, coriander, cumin, Worcestershire sauce, soy sauce, lime juice, orange juice, and paprika. Blend. Pour yogurt mixture over chicken and marinate in refrigerator for several hours. Remove chicken from marinade and broil until golden brown on each side.

Per serving
214 calories
58 mg cholesterol
155 mg sodium
1.37 gm saturated fat
6.3 gm fat

Exchanges per serving
½ fruit
2 meat
½ milk

On the side Saffron rice looks and tastes great with this dish. A mix of onions, mushrooms, and green peppers, sautéed with a little margarine, is our vegetable of choice. A fruit plate with yogurt dressing rounds out the meal nutritionally.

Texas-Style Chicken

Serves 8 **343**

1 Tbsp. peanut oil
1 lb. boneless, skinless chicken breasts
1 cup chopped onions
2 cups fresh chopped tomatoes
1 22-oz. can chili hot beans
⅔ cup oat bran
⅓ cup chopped red peppers
1 tsp. chili powder
1 tsp. minced garlic
1½ cup water
⅔ cup part-skim cheddar cheese, shredded

In skillet, heat oil. Cut chicken into thin slices and
sauté. Add remaining ingredients, except cheese, and
simmer for 25 to 30 minutes. Top with cheese and
cover until cheese melts.

Per serving
315 calories
58 mg cholesterol
359 mg sodium
3 gm saturated fat
8.8 gm fat

Exchanges per serving
1 bread
1 fat
2 meat
1 vegetable

On the side A cabbage salad, a glass of milk, and a fresh fruit for
dessert complete this zesty meal nutritionally.

2 Tbsp. vegetable oil

1 cup chopped walnuts

3 whole boned, skinned, chicken breasts, cubed

½ cup low-sodium chicken broth

1 Tbsp. cornstarch

1 Tbsp. water

3 tsp. soy sauce

⅛ tsp. pepper

In skillet, heat 1 tablespoon oil and fry walnuts, but don't brown them. Heat remaining oil and stir-fry chicken until browned. Add broth and cook on high heat for 5 minutes. In a bowl, combine cornstarch, water, soy sauce, and pepper. Stir in cornstarch mixture; stir until thickened. Add walnuts.

Per serving
334 calories
71 mg cholesterol
558 mg sodium
4.3 gm saturated fat
14.6 gm fat

Exchanges per serving
1 fat
3 meat

On the side This Walnut Chicken recipe goes well with white or brown rice, according to your preference. We also like to serve sautéed snow pea pods to enhance the oriental style of this dish. Add a glass of milk and a fresh fruit for dessert and the meal is complete nutritionally.

Apricot-Cornish Game Hens

2 (1½ lb) Cornish game hens, halved
2 Tbsp. Worcestershire sauce
1 tsp. soy sauce
1 Tbsp. cornstarch
⅔ cup unsweetened apricot nectar
1½ Tbsp. unsweetened apricot jam
1 orange, peeled and cut into pieces

Preheat oven to 350°F. Brush halved hens with
Worcestershire sauce and soy sauce; broil until lightly
browned on each side. Combine cornstarch, nectar,
and jam in saucepan and bring to a boil. Put hens in a
baking dish and pour sauce over them. Bake for 30 to
35 minutes. Sprinkle with orange pieces and bake for
2 to 3 minutes more.

Per serving
214 calories
63 mg cholesterol
348 mg sodium
0.5 gm saturated fat
7 gm fat

Exchanges per serving
1 fruit
2 meat

On the side Boiled squash adds a gourmet touch to these
delicious hens. Broccoli spears, steamed just until tender, and
a dessert of mixed fruit and yogurt complete the meal
nutritionally.

4 turkey breast tenderloins
1½ Tbsp. margarine, melted
1 Tbsp. soy sauce
¼ cup cranberry orange sauce
¼ cup orange juice
1 tsp. cornstarch
⅛ tsp. ground cinnamon
⅛ tsp. ground cloves

In a bowl, stir together margarine and soy sauce. Place turkey on broiler pan; brush with soy sauce mixture. Broil on both sides until turkey is tender; brush with soy sauce mixture occasionally. In a saucepan, add remaining ingredients. Cook and stir until thickened and bubbly. Spoon over turkey steaks.

Per serving
141 calories
9 mg cholesterol
322 mg sodium
0.95 gm saturated fat
5.0 gm fat

Exchanges per serving
½ fruit
2 meat

On the side Try twice-baked yams as the bread course, cherry tomatoes cooked gently in a little margarine and tossed with rosemary, as the vegetable course, and add a glass of milk and a fresh fruit for dessert to complete this meal nutritionally.

⅔ cup part-skim cottage cheese
½ cup skim milk
¼ tsp. lemon juice
1 tsp. curry powder
8 oz. skinned and boned, cooked turkey, sliced
⅛ tsp. pepper

In bowl, combine cottage cheese, milk, lemon juice and curry powder; mix with a mixer until smooth. In saucepan, heat cheese mixture, stirring constantly; bring to a boil. Add turkey until heated through. Sprinkle each serving with pepper.

Per serving
110 calories
32 mg cholesterol
132 mg sodium
1.3 gm saturated fat
3.0 gm fat

Exchanges per serving
2 meat

On the side Eggplant adds variety here for the bread course and works well with this curry-flavored turkey dish. A colorful mixed vegetable, like carrots and green beans, or broccoli and carrots, a glass of milk, and a fresh fruit for dessert round out the meal nutritionally.

½ cup low-fat plain yogurt
¼ cup light mayonnaise
1½ Tbsp. skim milk
1 tsp. curry powder
⅛ tsp. pepper
3 cups chopped cooked turkey
⅔ cup halved seedless grapes
⅓ cup chopped water chestnuts
½ cup chopped red peppers
⅛ tsp. nutmeg
6 lettuce leaves

In a bowl, combine yogurt, mayonnaise, milk, curry powder and pepper. Mix well. Fold in turkey, grapes, water chestnuts, and red peppers. Sprinkle with nutmeg. Serve on lettuce leaves.

Per serving
260 calories
21 mg cholesterol
409 mg sodium
4.9 gm saturated fat
8.1 gm fat

Exchanges per serving
1 fat
2 meat
1 vegetable

On the side We like to serve this terrific salad with a hearty rye or pumpernickel bread, a glass of milk, and fresh pear slices for dessert. The meal is delicious and is nutritionally complete.

1 cup diced celery
2 tsp. dried minced onion
1 Tbsp. margarine
2 cups water
½ tsp. salt
½ tsp. basil
¼ tsp. oregano
1 lb. can low-sodium tomatoes, reserve liquid
1 cup raw rice
2 5-oz. cans boned turkey

In skillet, combine celery, onion, margarine, water, salt, basil, oregano and liquid from tomatoes. Bring to a boil; add rice and bring to a second boil. Reduce heat and simmer until rice is done. Add tomatoes and turkey. Heat thoroughly.

Per serving
194 calories
22.2 mg cholesterol
324 mg sodium
0.9 gm saturated fat
3.7 gm fat

Exchanges per serving
½ bread
1½ meat
1 vegetable

On the side Add only a glass of milk, a ½ slice of bread, and a fruit of your choice for dessert and this meal is nutritionally complete.

350 Smoked Turkey with Vegetables

1½ cups chopped green pepper
1 cup chopped onions
1 cup chopped carrots
⅓ cup water
2 cups peeled, cooked potatoes, diced
12 oz. pre-cooked smoked turkey sausage, sliced

In skillet, combine green pepper, onion, and carrots with water; cover and cook until vegetables are tender-crisp. Add potatoes and sausage until heated through.

Per serving
283 calories
57 mg cholesterol
873 mg sodium
0.9 gm saturated fat
11.4 gm fat

Exchanges per serving
1 bread
3 meat
1 vegetable

On the side Serve with a glass of milk and a fresh fruit for dessert and you've got a nutritionally complete meal with this easy single dish.

1 Tbsp. vegetable oil
¾ cup diced celery
½ cup chopped onions
2 cups sliced, fresh mushrooms
1 Tbsp. cornstarch
¼ cup soy sauce
¾ cup cold water
¼ cup sliced water chestnuts
2 cups diced, cooked turkey
6 cups cooked rice

In skillet, heat oil. Add celery, onions, and mush-rooms; stir-fry until crisp-tender. In bowl, combine cornstarch, soy sauce, and water; mix. Stir cornstarch mixture into vegetables. Cook and stir constantly until liquid is smooth and thickened. Add water chestnuts and turkey. Cook until hot. Serve over rice.

Per serving
285 calories
32.3 mg cholesterol
735 mg sodium
0.7 gm saturated fat
4.1 gm fat

Exchanges per serving
1 bread
2 meat
1 vegetable

On the side You need only a glass of milk and a fresh fruit for dessert to make this quick and easy meal wholesome and nutritionally complete.

7 oz. ground turkey
⅓ cup chopped onions
1 cup tomatoes, chopped
⅔ cup low-sodium tomato sauce
½ cup water
2 tsp. chili powder
2 tsp. Worcestershire sauce
½ tsp. vinegar
½ tsp. garlic powder
⅛ tsp. allspice
1 tsp. crushed red pepper

In 3-quart saucepan, over medium heat, cook turkey and onions until turkey is brown. Add remaining ingredients and stir well to combine. Reduce heat and simmer for 30 minutes.

Per serving
262 calories
75 mg cholesterol
1408 mg sodium
1.05 gm saturated fat
13.97 gm fat

Exchanges per serving
3 meat
2 vegetable

On the side We like to serve this spicy chili recipe with elbow macaroni (½ cup servings are equal to 1 bread exchange and are about 150 calories; check the package for exact amounts). A glass of milk and apple-cranberry sauce complete the meal nutritionally.

1¼ lb. uncooked ground turkey
¼ cup chopped onions
1 cup tomato sauce
1 cup whole-wheat bread crumbs
2 eggs
1 tsp. oregano
1 tsp. basil
1 tsp. dry mustard
1 tsp. minced garlic
1½ cup frozen, chopped spinach, drained
½ cup mozzarella cheese, part-skim

Heat oven to 350°F. Combine turkey, onions, ¼ cup tomato sauce, bread crumbs, eggs, oregano, basil, mustard, and garlic; mix thoroughly. On a sheet of foil, pat mixture into a 12 x 8-inch rectangle. Spread spinach over turkey mixture; sprinkle with cheese. Roll turkey up starting on the 8-inch side. Place seam side down on cookie sheet. Bake 60 minutes. Heat remaining tomato sauce and spread over turkey roll.

Per serving
210 calories
104 mg cholesterol
308 mg sodium
1.75 gm saturated fat
4.8 gm fat

Exchanges per serving
½ bread
2 meat
1 vegetable

On the side Fresh tomato slices, arranged attractively on the plate with this dish, look and taste great. Add a glass of milk and fresh strawberries to complete your meal.

354 Sprouts 'n Turkey Pockets

1½ cups low-fat, plain yogurt
1 tsp. Dijon-style mustard
1 tsp. horseradish
2 whole-wheat pocket breads, halved
½ lb. sliced cooked turkey
¾ cup alfalfa sprouts
¾ cup chopped tomato

In a small bowl, combine 8 tablespoons yogurt, mustard, and horseradish; blend well. Spoon 2 tablespoons yogurt mixture into each pocket half. Fill each with ¼ of the turkey, sprouts and tomato. Serve with remaining yogurt.

Per serving
207 calories
47 mg cholesterol
227 mg sodium
1.5 gm saturated fat
4.0 gm fat

Exchanges per serving
½ bread
1 meat
½ skim milk

On the side We like to serve this pita-style sandwich with fresh cucumber slices. A glass of milk and fresh pear slices for dessert complete the meal nutritionally.

Stuffed Pitas

1½ Tbsp. margarine
10 oz. turkey sausage, cubed
⅓ cup diced onion
⅓ cup chopped green pepper
¾ cup sauerkraut, drained
½ tsp. prepared mustard
½ tsp. prepared horseradish
4 whole-wheat pita pockets

In skillet, heat margarine. Add turkey sausage and sauté. Add onions and green pepper and sauté until tender-crisp. Add sauerkraut, mustard, and horseradish, and cook until heated thoroughly. Fill each pita pocket with ¼ of sausage mixture.

Per serving
299 calories
48 mg cholesterol
1315 mg sodium
2.5 gm saturated fat
12.2 gm fat

Exchanges
1½ bread
1 fat
1 meat
1 vegetable

On the side Serve these hearty pita sandwiches with a dessert of plain nonfat yogurt gently mixed with your favorite fresh fruits or berries.

1 small cucumber
1 small carrot
4 oz. light cream cheese
2 Tbsp. skim milk
¼ cup chopped green onion
⅛ tsp. curry powder
1 Tbsp. chopped pimentos
4 6-inch flour tortillas
4 lettuce leaves
8 oz. thinly sliced smoked turkey

Cut cucumber and carrot into thinly sliced sticks. In a mixing bowl, stir together cream cheese, milk, onions, curry powder, and pimentos. Spread mixture on one side of each tortilla. Top with lettuce leaves, turkey, cucumber and carrots. Fold and secure with toothpicks.

Per serving
273 calories
65.5 mg cholesterol
459 mg sodium
0.5 gm saturated fat
13.25 gm fat

Exchanges per serving
1 bread
½ fat
2 meat

On the side These tortilla roll-ups look great on a plate next to a salad of mixed greens, red and green peppers, and onion slices. Serve a glass of milk and your choice of fruit (we like cantaloupe melon slices) and the meal is nutritionally complete.

1½ Tbsp. vegetable oil
2 lb. turkey roast, cubed
¼ cup flour
1 cup chopped onion
¾ cup chopped celery
1½ cups chopped carrots
1 can condensed consommé
½ cup water
⅓ cup burgundy wine
⅛ tsp. pepper
⅛ tsp. salt
¼ tsp. celery seed

In a skillet, heat oil. Lightly flour meat, and brown.
Add remaining ingredients, cover, and simmer until
meat is tender. Stir often.

Per serving
203 calories
60 mg cholesterol
1087 mg sodium
1.2 gm saturated fat
5.2 gm fat

Exchanges per serving
½ fat
3 meat
1 vegetable

On the side Mix green beans and carrots, steam them, and serve
them with a slice of bread and a glass of milk for a
nutritionally complete meal.

2 potatoes, peeled and cubed
½ cup chopped celery
3¼ cup skim milk
1 17-oz. can cream-style corn
2 4-oz. packages turkey breasts, cut into squares
¼ tsp. salt
⅛ tsp. pepper
¼ tsp. nutmeg

In saucepan, cook potatoes and celery in milk until potatoes are tender; mash slightly. Stir in corn, turkey, salt, pepper, and nutmeg. Simmer for 10 more minutes.

Per serving
449 calories
139 mg cholesterol
660 mg sodium
1.7 gm saturated fat
6.3 gm fat

Exchanges per serving
2 bread
1 fat
2 meat
1 skim milk

On the side This robust, dinner in a dish needs only a vegetable and a fruit to make the meal complete nutritionally. We like to make a Waldorf-style salad of mixed lettuce, cabbage, apples, celery, and raisins with a yogurt dressing, but cooked cabbage goes well with this dish, too.

Turkey in Creamy Orange Sauce

1 Tbsp. vegetable oil
12 oz. boneless, skinless turkey breasts
⅔ cup orange juice
1 tsp. cornstarch
⅔ cup low-fat plain yogurt
⅓ cup low-fat cottage cheese
⅛ tsp. black pepper

Heat oil in skillet and brown turkey on both sides. Mix orange juice and cornstarch and add to skillet; simmer to thicken and finish cooking turkey. Blend yogurt and cottage cheese until smooth. Stir into turkey mixture. Heat thoroughly, but do not boil. Season with pepper.

Per serving
340 calories
88 mg cholesterol
124 mg sodium
7.2 gm saturated fat
10.3 gm fat

Exchanges per serving
1 fat
4 meat

On the side A serving of white rice, refreshing chilled cucumber slices, and a dessert of yogurt gently blended with fresh Bing cherries make this an elegant dinner for two that's also nutritionally complete.

1 Tbsp. margarine
⅓ cup chopped green pepper
⅓ cup chopped onion
¼ cup chopped celery
1 cup chopped tomato
1 cup low-sodium chicken broth
⅔ cup long grain rice
¾ tsp. basil, crushed
¼ tsp. thyme, crushed
⅛ tsp. garlic powder
⅛ tsp. pepper
¼ tsp. hot pepper sauce
1 bay leaf
2 cups cooked turkey, cubed

In skillet, heat margarine; cook green pepper, onion, and celery until tender. Stir in tomatoes, broth, rice, basil, thyme, garlic powder, pepper, and hot pepper sauce. Add bay leaf. Bring to a boil. Reduce heat and simmer for 20 minutes or until rice is tender. Stir in turkey; cook until heated through. Discard bay leaf.

Per serving
312 calories
87 mg cholesterol
138 mg sodium
2.3 gm saturated fat
9 gm fat

Exchanges per serving
1 bread
1 fat
2 meat
1 vegetable

On the side This hearty meal needs only a glass of milk and a fresh fruit for nutritional balance.

Nonstick cooking spray
1¼ lb. ground turkey
¾ cup whole wheat bread crumbs
½ cup chopped onion
¼ cup diced celery
¼ cup chopped carrots
1 tsp. minced garlic
¼ cup skim milk
1 Tbsp. dried parsley flakes
1 egg
⅛ tsp. black pepper
1 tsp. Worcestershire sauce
1 tsp. dried dillweed
½ tsp. sage

Preheat oven to 350°F. Spray 9 x 15-inch loaf pan with nonstick cooking spray. In a large bowl, mix all ingredients; blend well. Spoon into pan and shape into a loaf. Bake 50 to 60 minutes until loaf pulls away from pan.

Per serving
211 calories
103 mg cholesterol
196 mg sodium
1.6 gm saturated fat
6.1 gm fat

Exchanges per serving
2 meat
1 vegetable

On the side For nutritional completeness, serve new potatoes with parsley, cooked carrots, a glass of milk, and we like our cranberry-apple sauce, but you may want a fruit of your choice.

10 oz. turkey breast
1 cup water
¼ cup finely chopped onion
2 tsp. ground ginger
2 Tbsp. soy sauce
3 tsp. Worcestershire sauce
1 tsp. garlic

In a blender, combine all ingredients, except turkey, and process until smooth. Place turkey in shallow pan and cover with sauce. Marinate for 1½ hours. Broil or grill turkey breast until done to taste. Heat marinade and serve with turkey.

Per serving
226 calories
83 mg cholesterol
1065 mg sodium
2.5 gm saturated fat
3 gm fat

Exchanges per serving
4 meat
½ vegetable

On the side Get a half-bunch of broccoli florets and steam them until they are tender to serve beside this tangy turkey dish. Some rice or a slice of bread, a glass of milk, and fresh pears for dessert complete the meal nutritionally.

Turkey Vegetable Skillet

1 lb. ground turkey
1 small onion, chopped
1 clove garlic, minced
1 tsp. olive oil
1 lb. fresh tomatoes, chopped
¼ lb. zucchini, diced
¼ cup chopped dill pickle
1 tsp. dried basil
½ tsp. pepper

In a skillet, brown turkey, onion, and garlic in oil. Add remaining ingredients. Simmer, uncovered, for 5 to 10 minutes or until the turkey is cooked and zucchini is tender.

Per serving
138 calories
28 mg cholesterol
196 mg sodium
1.7 gm saturated fat
6.6 gm fat

Exchanges per serving
1 vegetable
1 meat

On the side Steam mixed vegetables, and serve with a slice of bread and a glass of milk for a nutritionally complete meal.

Nonstick cooking spray
1 cup sliced celery
½ cup sliced carrots
1 cup skim milk, divided
2 Tbsp. cornstarch
¾ cup chicken broth
2 Tbsp. dried minced onion
½ tsp. garlic powder
2½ tsp. curry powder
2 cups cooked turkey
2½ cups cooked rice

Lightly coat a skillet with cooking spray; saute celery and carrots until tender. In a bowl, mix ¼ cup milk and cornstarch until smooth. Add broth and remaining milk. Mix until smooth. Pour over vegetables in skillet. Add onion, garlic powder and curry powder. Cook and stir over medium heat for 4 to 5 minutes or until mixture thickens and bubbles. Add turkey; cook and stir until heated through. Serve over rice.

Per serving
319 calories
38 mg cholesterol
391 mg sodium
1.1 gm saturated fat
3.6 gm fat

Exchanges per serving
3 meat
1 vegetable
2½ bread

On the side A glass of milk and a fresh fruit complete this meal nicely.

1 Tbsp. tomato paste
½ cup water
1 lb. ground turkey
1 egg
⅓ cup grated zucchini
⅓ cup grated carrots
½ tsp. thyme
⅓ cup bran
⅛ tsp. pepper
1 tsp. Worcestershire sauce
¼ cup grated part-skim Swiss cheese

Preheat oven to 350°F. In a bowl, mix tomato paste with water. Add remaining ingredients. Mix well. Shape into loaf and place in loaf pan. Bake for 1 hour.

Per serving
191 calories
109 mg cholesterol
131 mg sodium
2.6 gm saturated fat
9 gm fat

Exchanges per serving
3 meat

On the side Serve this hearty meat loaf with a baked potato, a glass of milk, and a serving of your favorite fruit for dessert for a nutritionally balanced meal.

INDEX

scampi, shrimp, 213
Scotch Chicken, 348
Seafood Casserole, 206
seafood and fish, 149-239
Sesame Shrimp Broil, 207
Sesame Shrimp, 208
sherry mushroom sauce, fish
    fillets in, 170
Shrimp and Pea Salad, 27
Shrimp and Rice Chowder,
    47
Shrimp Creole, 209
Shrimp in Garlic Butter, 210
Shrimp Kabob, 211
Shrimp Oriental, 212
Shrimp Salad Pocket, 54
Shrimp Salad, 28
Shrimp Scampi, 213
Shrimp Stuffed Pitas, 55
shrimp
    and scallops, broiled, 201
    broil, sesame, 207
    salad, tarragon, 31
shrimp,
    baked, 200
    coriander, 202
    creole, 203
    curried, 204
    hot, 205
    sesame, 208
Simple Salmon, 192
Smoked Turkey with
    Vegetables, 366
Snapper with Mushrooms,
    216
snapper,
    poached red, 214
    spicy, 215
Sole with Wine, 186
sole fillets,
    broiled, 178
    crunchy, 179
sole,
    baked fillet of, 172
    Oriental-style, 182
    ricotta, 185
soufflé,
    tuna, 231
    vegetable, 108
soups, 39-48

Spaghetti with Peas and
    Tomato Sauce, 79
spaghetti toss, asparagus, 64
spaghetti,
    summer, 82
    vegetable, 85
Spanish Chicken Bake, 349
Spicy Baked Chicken, 350
Spicy Chicken, 351
Spicy Oven-Fried Chicken,
    352
Spicy Snapper, 215
Spicy Turkey Chili, 368
Spinach Fruit Salad, 29
Spinach Tortellini with
    Tomato-Vegetable Sauce,
    80
Spinach Turkey Roll, 369
Spinach Turkey Salad, 30
spinach
    casserole, squash and,
    101
    fettuccine, herbed, 67
    salad, pasta, 24
spinach,
    chicken with, 303
    lemon veal with, 132
Split Pea Soup, 48
Sprout Sandwich, 56
Sprouts 'n Turkey Pockets,
    370
Squash and Spinach
    Casserole, 101
steak stew, quick, 136
steak,
    barbecued flank, 116
    dilled round, 123
    green pepper, 130
    mushroom veal, 134
steaks à la citrus, halibut,
    169
stew,
    delicious easy oven, 122
    pasta bean, 71
    quick steak, 136
    veal barley, 143
Stir Fry Vegetables, 102
Stir-Fried Chicken, 353